MICHELIN MAN

100 YEARS OF BIBENDUM

Olivier Darmon

Translated from the French
by Bernard Besserglik

conran
OCTOPUS

First published in Great Britain
in 1998 by Conran Octopus Limited
37 Shelton Street
London WC2H 9HN

Originally published in English as
One Hundred Years of Michelin Man by
Editions Hoëbeke, Paris, 1997
© Editions Hoëbeke, Paris 1997

Jacket design and layout copyright
© Conran Octopus 1998

ISBN 1 84091 031 3

Artwork: Massin
Jacket Design: Alison Fenton
Archives: Michelin
Photography: Michel Kempf
Translation: Multilingue
Revision: Barry Tulett
Typesetting: Traitext
Photoengraving: Prodima

British Library Cataloguing-in-
Publication Data
A catalogue record for this book is
available from the British library

Printed in Italy

Chapter 1

Before Bibendum

Le Petit Journal

SUPPLÉMENT ILLUSTRÉ

TOUS LES VENDREDIS
Le Supplément illustré
5 Centimes

Huit pages : CINQ centimes

TOUS LES JOURS
Le Petit Journal
5 Centimes

Deuxième Année   SAMEDI 26 SEPTEMBRE 1891   Numéro 44

M. CHARLES TERRONT
Vainqueur de la course nationale de Paris à Brest
organisée par le « Petit Journal »

6

Prologue: Paris-Brest-Paris, the path to glory

Five o'clock on Sunday morning, September 6, 1891: a strange time for a crowd to be gathering in Montholon square, filing through the streets of northern Paris to cluster around the offices of the popular newspaper *Le Petit Journal*, located at 61 rue La Fayette. But then this is no ordinary Sunday. Today, about an hour from now, marks the start of an historic event, a cycle race from Paris to Brest and back, a round trip between the capital and the Atlantic coast of 800 miles. The police are out in force, politely and good-naturedly shepherding the crowd of enthusiasts, friends and curious bystanders, making sure the holiday mood remains within the bounds defined by law.

For this is the moment everyone has been waiting for, ever since, several months ago, *Le Petit Journal* first announced that it was organising something as unheard of as a Paris-Brest cycle race. Not content to rest on the laurels of its million-plus circulation, the paper had chosen this means of boosting its prestige further. Apart from the publicity it provided, the race would be an excellent method for assessing the impact the newspaper had on its readers and the popular passion for the new sport of cycle racing. Himself a recent convert, editor Pierre Giffard hoped devoutly that the event, which he had taken upon himself to organise, would prove a success. The cycle industry needed the boost. Its products had yet to acquire a reputation for reliability. This could be its big chance. As he wrote in his editorial for that memorable day:

"Yes, once again we've organised a cycle race for you. Maybe it will be this race that produces, at last, the bike that does not go wrong -- as eight out of ten of the bikes sold under that name tend to do. What progress that would be for cycling, if such were to be the case!"

Indeed, it is not human endurance that is to be put to the test in the coming marathon, but rather that of the machines. The rules specify quite clearly that the entire course of the race is to be ridden on the same bicycle. This is no doubt why the most anxious of the many hundreds of people milling around the 206 riders and their trainers are the bicycle manufacturers. In those days the industry still comprised scores of small businesses, many of them using ramshackle methods. Each company boss is there, fussily making sure that his rider has everything he needs to achieve optimum performance. Among them are two brothers, André and Edouard Michelin, fledgling

entrepreneurs with something to prove: as inventors of the new detachable Michelin tyre, they see the Paris-Brest round trip as the ideal opportunity to establish their product's superiority on its first official outing. They have engaged champion cyclist Charles Terront to maximise their chances of carrying off the prize.

At 6.17 a.m. precisely, Pierre Giffard steps forward and gives a signal. A dozen klaxons ring out from the balcony of *Le Petit Journal*, and the race has begun. Like a swarm of bees the competitors rush down the rue La Fayette until they reach the Grands Boulevards and head for the Champs-Elysées, finally disappearing into the Bois de Boulogne. In those long-gone Victorian times cycling was still regarded as some strange game of skill, or at best as a rich man's hobby, and the idea of long-distance racing appeared a bizarre extravagance to all but a minority of aficionados. This tiny band of brothers knew everything it was possible to know about racing records and the exploits of champions past. In the view of the experts, two men stood head and shoulders above the rest: Joseph Laval from Bordeaux, popularly known as "J.L.", and Charles Terront, from the northern suburbs of Paris. And the experts were right, for "J.L." and Terront raced into an early lead and stayed out in front, fighting it out between them for the rest of the contest.

Terront, wearing armband number five, struck out on his own and maintained his advantage as far as Morlaix, 40 miles short of Brest. But then something strange happened: he disappeared. "J.L." made his triumphal entry into the Brittany port city, leaving Terront's supporters wondering what had become of their hero. The drama

Page 6: Charles Terront on the front page of the illustrated supplement of Le Petit Journal. As winner of the Paris-Brest-Paris cycle race he became, in 1891, the first sportsman to become a national celebrity and, in 1893, to publish his memoirs.
Above: Charles Terront on the Humber cycle on which he won the race. Weighing 47 pounds (compared with 20 pounds for today's racing cycles), it was fitted with detachable Michelin air-filled tyres.

heightened further when a rumour swept the crowd: "Terront is dead!" The city was ablaze with speculation -- had "Charley", as he was affectionately known by his British trainer, traded in his two wheels for wings and a harp? -- Finally the truth emerged in the form of a news report from Morlaix: Terront had taken an enforced break because of a puncture. "Having punctured his tyre six miles out of Morlaix, Terront will be arriving at Brest 42 minutes later than planned", the correspondent of *Le Petit Journal* reported. "He does not appear more tired than his rival and there is no tremor in his voice when he speaks," he added. Thirty-five hours' hard pedalling and "so far neither J.L. nor Terront has had to take to his bed".

Over the no less eventful return journey, and following a third sleepless night, Terront remorselessly built up an eight-hour lead over his adversary, passing La Queue-lès-Yvelines, a few miles west of Paris, with the race in his pocket. With his legs starting to give way, "J.L." decided he had no choice but to rest during the night. As he passed through the check-point the following morning, he feigned an air of indifference: "He calmly knocked back a concoction of eggs whipped in Madeira wine, browsing through the latest edition of *Le Petit Journal*", according to one report. And so at 6.35 in the morning of September 9, Terront crossed the winning line on the boulevard Maillot, opposite the Gillet restaurant. He had completed the first Paris-Brest-Paris race in a shade under three days: to be precise, in 71 hours and 18 minutes. "J.L.", the runner-up, strolled home nine hours later, by

which time most of the 10,000 spectators who had turned out to acclaim the winner had dispersed. Terront had already became legendary.

This was "Charley's" greatest victory, the apotheosis of a long and illustrious career which was drawing to a close. The stocky yet lithe and powerful cyclist was to hang up his handle-bars for good three years later, aged 34, after completing the Saint Petersburg-Paris race. Among his many laurels were victories in the first two six-day events in the United States in 1879, in track events in London and Edinburgh in 1880 -- for which he earned the nickname "Napo-Terront" -- and in the French 100-kilometre championship in 1880. He was the first cyclist to become a household name nationally. And Terront never forgot the debt he owed to the Michelin brothers.

"We paid a visit to the winner and he attributed his success to the pneumatic tyre he was using", *Le Figaro* reported on September 10. The tribute was no doubt sincere but gave no indication of the behind-the-scenes drama that had preceded the race. Several months earlier, the Michelin brothers had secured Terront's agreement to represent them. The agreement was reached after a lavish meal, washed down with the best wines, followed by a short trial of the new tyre to convince the champion of the technical interest of the invention. Previously they had attempted to recruit "J.L." Laval, the favourite then under contract to Dunlop, but failed for a very good reason: their ground-breaking new detachable tyre existed only on paper. André and Edouard Michelin

Rencontre d'un troupeau de bestiaux.

Above, from top down: *The main actors in the legendary Paris-Brest-Paris cycle race -- organiser Pierre Giffard, and the leading competitors, Charles Terront and Joseph Laval. "The hazards of the journey", a contemporary engraving.*
Page 9: *"The air-filled tyre is, and by its nature always will be, faster than other tyres" -- the leaflet by Michelin distributed at the finishing line of the Paris-Brest race. A contemporary engraving illustrating an account of the race, and showing the poor state of the roads at that time.*

distributing brochures within minutes of his crossing the line. Written and printed overnight, when the inevitablity of Terront's victory became apparent, the publicity material was handed out even as the crowds were milling around to shake the champion's hand. The brochure informed the public of the advantages of the pneumatic tyre, and pressed home its point with a humourous anecdote typical of the period:

"Louis XVI, on being informed by the Marquis de La Fayette that the Bastille had fallen to the insurgents, exclaimed: 'Good heavens! Is this a revolt?' 'No Sire,' the marquis replied. 'It is a REVOLUTION.'

In the event that the bicycle-riding public, on learning of our new tyre, should exclaim: 'Good heavens! Is this an improvement?', we have no hesitation in replying: 'No -- it is a REVOLUTION.'"

The next stage in the Michelin publicity offensive was a simple statement published in the specialist cycling magazine *Vélo Sport*. A discreet three-inch-high box at the bottom of the page announced modestly:

were bidding for the services of a leading athlete over the most demanding course in the racing calendar without even being sure that they could provide the necessary material. Circumstances had forced them to gamble, to innovate in a race against time. Testimony, if nothing else, to the determination and the ambition of the two brothers. And a turning point in the career of Michelin & Co as the inexperienced but nevertheless dynamic duo sought to pull away from the pack.

The Michelin brothers lost no time in making the most of Charles Terront's achievement. In a move that impresses even now for its decisiveness, they set about

PARIS. — LA GRANDE COURSE DE BICYCLETTES DE PARIS-BREST-PARIS; L'ARRIVÉE DU VAINQUEUR, M. CH. TERRONT, A LA PORTE MAILLOT. — (Dessin de M. P. Carrey.) — Voir page 457.

1. M. Ch. Terront, le gagnant de la course Paris-Brest-Paris (Photographie Tillier, à Angers). — 2. M. Jiel-Laval, arrivé second. — 3. Arrivée de M. Ch. Terront à la porte Mai
4. Son entrée au contrôle. — 5. Vive Terront! — 6. Sur la grande route pendant la nuit.

"Michelin tyres, Clermont-Ferrand.

Easy to remove and repair, their tyre enabled me to win the Paris-Brest. Signed: Charles Terront."

This small beginning in relations with the press was followed up with a letter to the editor of *Le Petit Journal*, published on page 2:

"Dear Sir,

It was your paper's interest in cycling matters that induced us to concentrate our efforts in that direction. It was on account of the Paris-Brest race, in order to meet its requirements, that we invented our detachable pneumatic tyre.

You were the essential reason for our invention and we would like to express our gratitude.

In return we would like to give the widest circulation to your excellent idea. (...) Cycle races are an ideal means of putting the latest innovations to the test.

In order to facilitate comparisons and following your example, we propose to organise a race in which all bicycles will be fitted with our detachable rubber tyres.

The race is open to French amateur cyclists and will follow the route Clermont-Ferrand to Paris, starting in the third week of October.

(...) You have done so much for practical cycling, Sir, that it is to you that we wish, so to speak, to dedicate this new competition.

With our sincerest best wishes,

Michelin & Co
Clermont-Ferrand

PS. Details and conditions concerning the competition may be obtained by writing to Michelin & Co."

This respectful, reverential and yet vibrant profession of faith is typical of the brothers' ability to strike a popular chord. It not only provides the closing note to their publicity campaign based on Terront's victory; it also looks ahead to the theme they will adopt for subsequent competitions. This is to be seen as a natural extension of the research process, the ultimate test of the company's products in extreme and unpredictable conditions: a means as much as an end in itself. Sensitive to flattery, the newspaper printed the brothers' letter in full, providing them with some very welcome publicity and paying involuntary tribute to their talent for public relations. A talent that was to blossom in the years to come...

Apprenticeship

That the name of Michelin should become synonymous with rubber tyres owes as much to chance as to design. The origins of the company go back to 1832 when the brothers' maternal grandfather, Aristide Barbier, joined his cousin and friend Edouard Daubrée in setting up a rubber and agricultural goods company in the southern city of Clermont-Ferrand. After their deaths the company went into steep decline, under the incompetent management first of an heir then of an ill-chosen partner. By 1886 when André Michelin, then aged 33, took over the firm, it was on the brink of collapse.

Michelin's first priority was to hold on to the dwindling number of clients. But he also had to think about the future -- promoting existing products, developing new markets, rationalising production: in short, investing money and devoting himself entirely to the company, which for the moment was still in intensive care. It would have helped if he had known a little more about rubber...

*Page 10: Key events in the Paris-Brest race as seen by an artist at the time.
Above: Expanding rapidly in the last years of the century, the bicycle market was extremely competitive, as can be seen from this page of advertising in the magazine Le Cycle. The layout, an unimaginative pattern of slabs, would nowadays be considered totally uncommercial.*

André Michelin, a brilliant engineer specialising in architecture, had to admit he could hardly hope to succeed in running the company on his own. Particularly since his spiritual home was Paris, where he had set up his own firm specialising in metal structures. His heroes were Victor Baltard, whose cast-iron frames formed the infrastructure for the city's "belly", the Halles de Paris; Charles Boileau, whose graceful wrought-iron lattice-work was on display at the Bon Marché department store; Jules Saulnier, who

had just completed the Meunier chocolate factory in Noisiel, near Paris, a bold reinterpretation of mediaeval architecture in iron; Gustave Eiffel -- a graduate of the same school as André -- whose controversial, soon-to-be-world-famous tower was starting to rise above the Champ de Mars in western Paris, and other artists of the architectural avant-garde. No -- how could André leave Paris at such an exciting time as this?

But then there was Edouard. Less well established than André, his younger brother had just completed his fine arts studies and launched himself on a career as an artist under the guidance of his idol William Bouguereau. He had only lately set himself up at the Académie Jullian, at 5 rue Fromentin at the foot of Montmartre, and at the age of 29 was in pursuit of the Truth of Beauty. As a disciple of one of the masters of "official" painting, as opposed to Monet, Pissaro and other leading impressionists, Edouard had set his sights on perfection. There was little to suggest he would be disposed to setting up shop in the provinces.

How André succeeded in persuading Edouard to give up his paint brushes remains a mystery, though the negotiations must have been long and arduous, and Edouard's decision taken after heart-wrenching reflection. On May 28 1889 Edouard became -- almost certainly to his great surprise -- sole managing director of the company now trading under the name Michelin et Cie. "Master",

he told his artistic mentor, "my duty now is to go to Clermont to save the family firm from ruin. Though it pains me to renounce my art, I have thought it over at great length and I see where my duty lies". Bouguereau was no less pained to lose a disciple who, he said later, "paints like a pig but draws like an angel". He must have been hoping secretly that Edouard would fail to adjust to life in the provinces and would return in time to his first love.

"The navel is the eye of the body." This quotation by Ingres, emblazoned in large letters in Bouguereau's atelier, probably meant less to Edouard Michelin as he prepared for a new life as a rubber industrialist than the other lesson that his mentor had regularly drilled into him. "Perseverance! Perseverance is what gets results", the stocky painting master would insist, rolling his broad shoulders as he passed from one pupil to another. Perseverance was indeed the quality that the young would-be painter would need most in his unexpected new role as saviour of the fast-fading family firm out in the wilds of Clermont-Ferrand.

Miracles were in short supply as Edouard settled into his task, but he stuck to it, learning on the job, above all by listening to what his employees had to say.

"My first priority was to learn what the job was about", he recounted later. "The only way I could do this was to talk to the workers. I had to be in constant conversation with them, even though I knew far less than they did, and

the best way to get them talking was to admit openly that I was a complete beginner.

"I questioned them as if I was just having a friendly conversation, saying things like: How are you going to do that? Isn't there another way of doing it? Why not look for another way?

"In effect, I was trying to get

the worker, in this friendly chat, to convey all the experience he had acquired over the past 10, 20 or 30 years working in the factory."

Under its new management Michelin progressed slowly and hesitantly, adopting pragmatic policies based on constant observation of manufacturing techniques. Again, the painter Bouguereau had provided an adage that applied just as well to industry as it did to art. Attentiveness, he held, was the key to intelligence. Capable of spending hours in front of a flower, or gazing at a cloud, he told his students: "Ignorance makes you blind and lack of attention makes you ignorant; lack of attentiveness is stupid". Here too, Edouard had cause to thank his former master.

In its early days the Michelin company varied its production considerably, turning out valves, water or gas pipes, joints, belts and other motor-related items. Sales were modest, apart from two products which achieved a relatively high degree of popularity. The first of these was a child's rubber ball, an item that had formed part of the company's repertoire at its inception some six decades earlier, at the initiative of Edouard Daubrée's wife, Elisabeth Pugh Barker, niece of chemist Charles Mackintosh, famous for his invention in 1823 of the technique for waterproofing textiles. Between 1888 and 1894 orders for these small

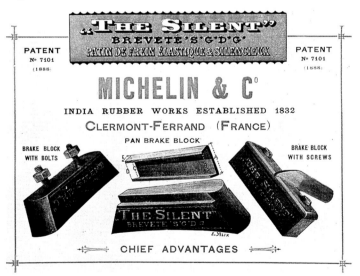

black balls from schools and other educational establishments increased 26-fold thanks to a vigorous sales policy aimed at finding new customers and boosting sales to exist-

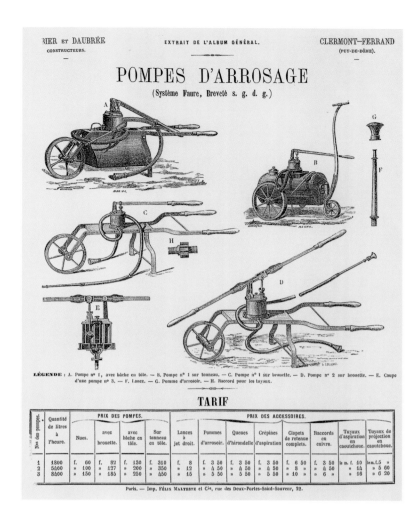

ing ones. The second best-seller was a new brake-pad called "The Silent", presented at the Universal Exhibition of 1889. This struck an immediate chord with the public, since brake-pads until then had been made of iron and emitted an infernal shriek during braking, to the great discomfort of riders. The Michelin innovation was to make the pad using rubber and canvas, providing the aural relief indicated by its name.

The Detachable

One spring-time afternoon in 1889, an ox-drawn cart clatters into the Michelin factory yard carrying a cyclist with a problem: one of the tyres of his bicycle has punctured. His mount is fitted with the latest Dunlop "sausage" -- the recently patented "rubber tube inflated with air and protected by fabric". Devised by Scottish businessman John Boyd Dunlop, the inflatable tyre represented a huge advance on its predecessor, the solid tyre which, justly nicknamed the "bone-shaker", would have the cyclist bouncing painfully in the saddle at the slightest bump in the road. However, it had the major drawback of being glued solidly to the rim of the wheel, so that in the event of a puncture the rider had to go through a complicated rigmarole involving innumerable tools and a 60-page repair instruction manual.

The Michelin workers, intrigued by this unusual tube of compressed air, set to work with a will to help out the

Page 12, from top down and from left to right: *Edouard Michelin. A moving portrait of the two brothers around 1885 (Edouard nearer the camera). André Michelin around 1890. Edouard Michelin with his workers, 1890.*
Above, from left to right: *the rubber brake-pad dubbed "The Silent", which appeared in 1889, was one of the company's first successes. Founded in 1832, the Barbier-Daubrée company became Michelin et Cie in May 1889.*

stricken cyclist. The repair was completed within three hours. However, the cyclist would have to wait until the following morning for the glue to dry. The next day Edouard, unable to resist the temptation to sample the pleasures of the inflatable tyre, set off for a spin through the streets of Clermont-Ferrand. Minutes later he was back -- on foot. The repair had failed the test of a short ride over the city's cobbled streets.

History does not tell us when the cyclist was eventually able to get on the way. Suffice it to say that his arrival in the factory yard marks the beginning of Edouard Michelin's keen interest in the development and improvement of the tyre. From this time on, all the company' s efforts were focused on tyre development, mobilising all the firm' s resources so that within a few years it had achieved astonishing growth.

Brief though it was, Edouard Michelin's excursion had been a revelation. Faster, more comfortable, easier to handle, in other words more effective than solid tyres, the inflatable tyre, he now saw, represented the future, though on one condition: that it be made easy to repair. The task

Le Cycle

Paris — 197, Boulevard Saint-Germain, 197 — Paris.

M. MICHELIN
Le père des pneumatiques démontables.

now was to work out a system of repair that would enable a cyclist "to replace an inner tube within a quarter of an hour, by simple means and without the need for a specialist... In other words, a detachable tyre which the layman can repair on his own and without fuss.".

A. MICHELIN
115, rue de Bagnolet, PARIS
PORTE EN FER FORGÉ

Achieving this became the company's absolute priority, its holy grail. It was by no means as straightforward a task as might be believed today. Separating the rim of the wheel from the band of material on which it turned ran counter to all the orthodoxies of the day. This, however, was the task to which Edouard Michelin and his engineer Laroche devoted all their efforts. It took them two years of hard work, two years of fumbling trial and error that culminated in applications for three patents during the summer of 1891, the third of them dated August 14, 1891, meeting their deadline -- the start of the Paris-Brest-Paris cycle race -- with just 24 days to spare.

The triumph of Michelin's Detachable tyre, thanks to the sterling efforts of Charles Terront, brought the firm renown its management had been hoping for and sealed its

destiny as a tyre manufacturer. The outstanding success of André Michelin's publicity also set the seal on the division of labour that the two brothers were henceforth to conform to: André, in Paris, abandoning his architectural interests, would be the company's marketing and public relations genius, while Edouard, in Clermont-Ferrand, would be head of research and oversee the production process. In short, the artist became the technical specialist, while the engineer proved his aptitude for sales. Whatever the apparent incongruities, this was the formula which was to found what in time would become the Michelin empire, with successive innovations rapidly finding their markets all over the world.

Though the first Detachable marked a huge advance on what had gone before, heralding the age of the practical inflatable tyre, there was still considerable scope for

Left: *Prospectus for the metal structures company formed by André Michelin who designed, among other things, the structures at the Peugeot factories at Valentigney, the Félix Potin building in Paris, and the spires of Saigon Cathedral.*
Right: *Edouard Michelin, "the father of the detachable tyre", cover of the magazine* Le Cycle, *June 1894.*
Page 15: *Taking the rim and the tyre as two distinct elements, Michelin designed the "Detachable".*

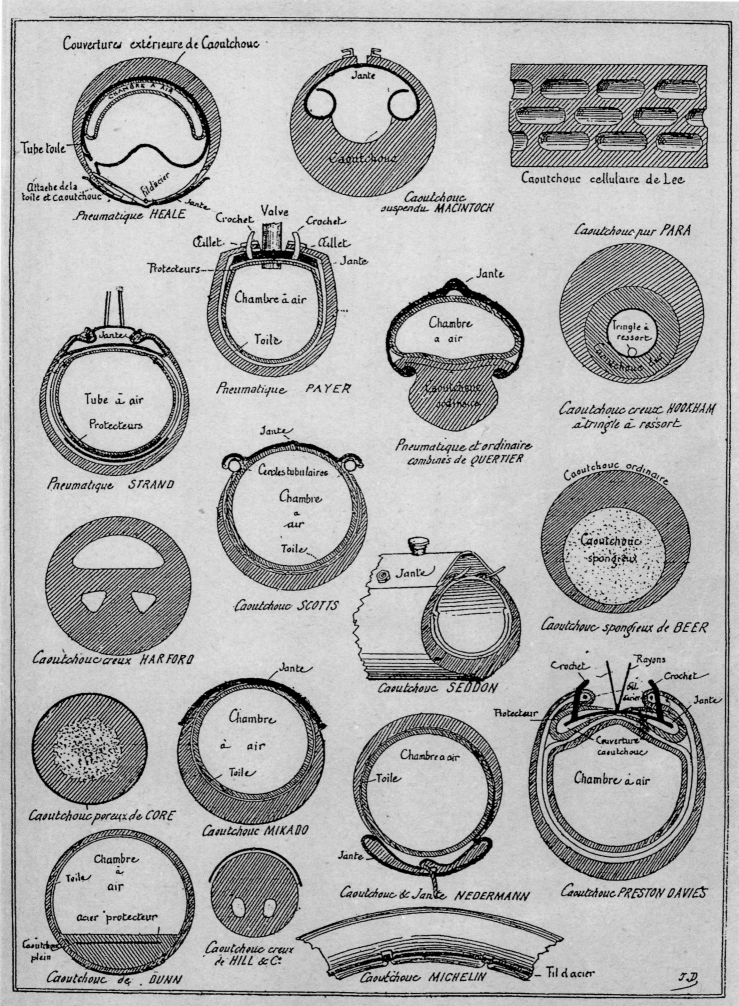

QUELQUES TYPES DE CAOUTCHOUCS AU STANLEY SHOW

Between 1895 and 1905 the company expanded rapidly. The factory in Clermont-Ferrand saw constant growth, the number of workers increasing from under three hundred to more than 3,000.
Above: *The factory gates.*
Below: *View of Clermont-Ferrand, around 1900.*
Page 16, from top down: *Extension of the Clermont-Ferrand factory in 1898.* Right: *Coal storage facilities. The Michelin factory and the tyre production workshop around 1900.*

476. CLERMONT-FERRAND (P.-de-D)   Usine Michelin

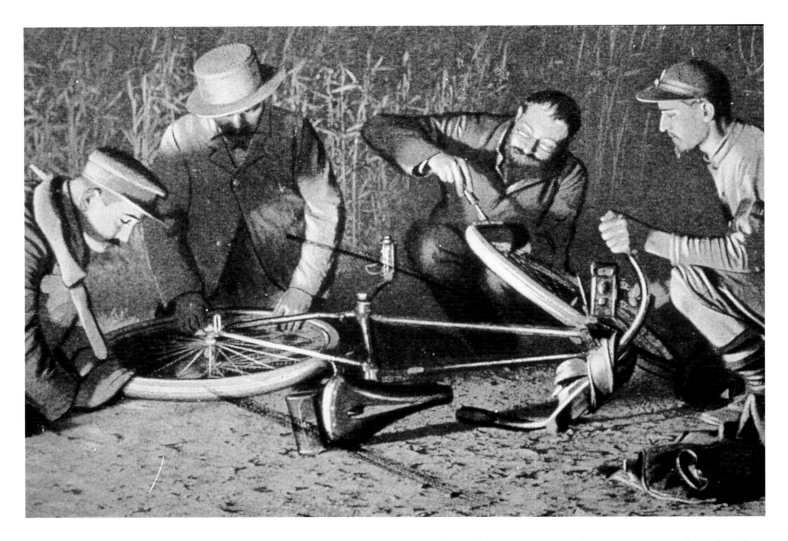

improvement. As Terront himself discovered to his cost, the time needed to undo the 17 screws involved in repairing a puncture was incompatible with winning cycle races. This is why, three months after Terront's victory in the Paris-Brest, Edouard Michelin had already perfected a new Detachable which reduced puncture repair times to levels comparable to those prevailing today. By December 1891 it was on display on the Michelin stand at the annual Stanley Cycle Show in London, the event's star attraction and the focus of André's considerable promotional talents.

A Michelin technician was at hand to show how the tyre could be removed at will in just one minute and 55 seconds. Rival exhibitors watched in envy as members of the public were invited onstage to try their hand at repeating the operation. Most managed it in two minutes or so; even the clumsiest took barely four minutes. The future of the Detachable was henceforth assured. Within days, and for some time to come, demand for the new tyre far outstripped Michelin's production capacity. This was success beyond the brothers' wildest dreams, but even so their adventure was only just beginning. Their eyes were already turned towards another invention of the future, one that promised to double their long-term sales prospects at the very least. For the motor car, as we all know, runs on twice as many wheels as the bicycle, without even counting the spare wheel, which was not introduced until after the First World War.

Edouard Michelin (centre) repairing a tyre during the Paris to Clermont-Ferrand race. It was important to show that punctures, the major disadvantage of pneumatic tyres in relation to solid ones, were really nothing to worry about. That is why Michelin organised this bicycle race on 5 June 1892, in which, unknown to the competitors, the firm scattered nails along the course in order to demonstrate that repairing of the company's tyres was now easy.

Chapter 2
Bibendum
is
born

The "horseless" carriage

As the 19th century draws to a close, a handful of engineers, mostly French and German, are busy pursuing the same dream. They are engaged, to the indifference of their fellow citizens, in laborious and complex work aimed at inventing a form of "new locomotion". Their efforts appear vain, almost comical. Their ingenious contraptions -- tricycles, quadricycles, steam or petroleum-driven carriages -- arouse more mirth than enthusiasm. When one of them succeeds in working up a speed of more than eight miles an hour, it is an event worthy of remark. And then there is the problem of steering. A driver has to be able to avoid crashing into a brick wall, the fate of Carl Benz in 1886 when he took his motorised tricycle on its first trial run. However risible, not to say dangerous, they may have appeared at the time, these early efforts to achieve "horseless" locomotion proved decisive for the future of transport. The names of the pioneers, notably Amédée Bollée, Gottlieb Daimler, Siegfried Marcus, Nikolaus Otto, Carl Benz, René Panhard, Emile Levassor, Armand Peugeot and Albert de Dion, have long since entered the hall of motoring fame.

and the northern French city of Rouen. Sponsored by the newspaper, this competition -- not, properly speaking, a race -- is the first of its kind in history, an event with a specific purpose. Its aim is to assess the potential of the various vehicles in the running, to sort out the viable projects with a future from the hare-brained schemes sprung from the fevered imaginings of a thousand inspired amateurs.

Despite the non-returnable entry fee set at a level "to deter the jokers seeking to pass themselves off as real inventors", the list of starters included vehicles driven by the most off-beat methods conceivable: systems of levers and rods that used the passenger's weight as the driving force, "electro-pneumatic" engines, combined "gas and gravity" engines, "compressed water" engines. A plethora of brilliant devices which, however, failed to get beyond the preliminary stages. Taking part as a passenger in a motorised omnibus invented by the ingenious blacksmith Léon Serpollet, André Michelin had a front row seat for observing this bizarre spectacle. Now, he concluded, was the moment of truth.

The day of the race, July 22, 1894, and only 21 vehicles have made it as far as the starting line. By an irony of fate

But for now they are still dreamers, a collection of ambitious inventors attempting to endow their machines with a degree of autonomy and reliability. Pierre Giffard, the enterprising editor of *Le Petit Journal*, decides in 1894 to allow them to test their inventions against each other by organising a motor "competition" between Paris

-- or perhaps through an act of perversity on the part of the organisers -- the course presents a major pitfall: part of the road is still waiting to be resurfaced and currently forms a quagmire in which vehicles with solid tyres are certain to founder. The situation provides hours of harmless fun for the spectators, watching the contestants attempting to haul their vehicles clear by means of ropes, and occasionally lending them a hand. The winner, a steam-powered estate car designed by De Dion, covers the 70-mile route at an

Page 20: The arrival of the first motor cars in the remote provinces at the turn of the century was seen as a cataclysm and a cause for fear, as vividly portrayed in this drawing by Léandre (1862-1934).
Above, left: Edouard Michelin has air-filled tyres fitted to one of the first motor-cars in 1895. Right: Tyres being changed in front of Michelin's head office in Paris, Boulevard Pereire.

21

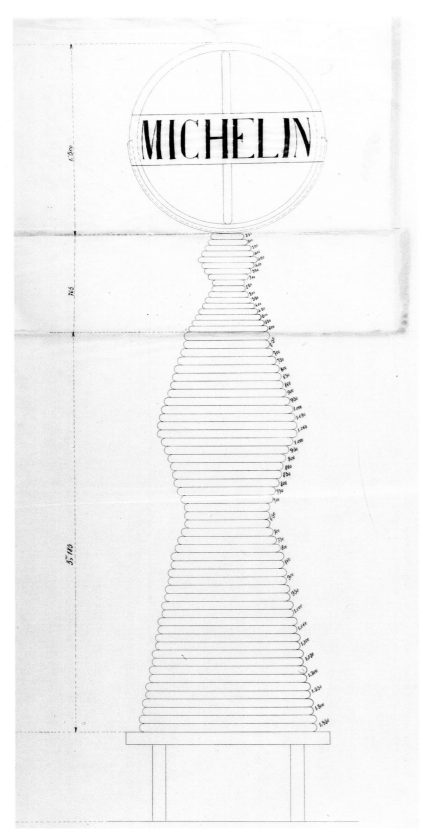

of towns along the way", wrote W. de Fonvielle in the *Journal des Connaissances Utiles*. "Everyone was delighted to see such a wide variety of types of machine, all capable of producing speed greater than that of horses, and with remarkable regularity." The press was unanimous in its fervent approval. "We have great faith in the considerable services that these mechanical vehicles are destined to provide", averred *L'Illustration*. And *Le Génie Civil* predicted: "The new vehicle is bound to have a profound effect on our habits of locomotion and our transport industry".

The task now for Michelin and Co. was to convince those modern heroes, the veterans of the Paris-Rouen race, of the virtues of the company's products. Car makers had until now opted for the same kind of wheel as those used on horse-drawn vehicles, that is to say a wooden wheel with a metal rim or a solid tyre, and showed no inclination to change. Their caution, or "obstinate scepticism" in the words of André Michelin, regarding the inflatable tyre was a matter of regret but had no immediate effect on the company's fortunes, since vehicle production as yet remained minute. In 1894 there were still barely 200 vehicles on French roads. There were a great many more bicycles, and the demand among the cycling public for Michelin tyres was sufficient to ensure the company's prosperity.

Turnover had quadrupled since the Paris-Brest race, and the factory in Clermont-Ferrand now employed 268 workers. The company had diversified, providing tyres for wheel-chairs and stretcher vehicles used in hospitals, for wheel-barrows and children's cars. The brake-pads known as "The Silent" -- a regular attraction at cycle shows -- now featured alongside the piles of tyres of various diameters which, stacked up one on top of the other, were to inspire the creation of the round, rubber figure who in time became the firm's mascot.

One day in 1894 the two Michelin brothers were visiting the Universal and Colonial Exhibition in Lyons. Looking for an original way of presenting the company's products, the organiser of the Michelin stand had placed two piles of tyres at the entrance. Edouard pointed to them and said to his brother: "Look at that. Add some arms, and you'd say they were men". A short time later André was visited by the graphic artist O'Galop. One of the advertising designs the artist had to show him portrayed, in caricature, a figure resembling Gambrinus, the king who, it is said, invented beer-brewing. It showed his outsize silhouette seated at a table, holding up a flagon of beer and exclaiming in Latin: "Nunc est bibendum" -- Now is the time to drink! The

average speed of 13 miles per hour, barely two miles an hour faster than Terront's performance by bike over a course 10 times as long. For André Michelin, however, despite the blisters caused by rope-pulling, it has been a memorable day. He returns to Paris fired with enthusiasm, convinced that the "new locomotion" has a brilliant future -- provided that someone comes up with the right kind of tyres.

Like the Paris-Brest, the Paris-Rouen event was a huge success, "giving rise to high emotions among the residents design, which O'Galop had unsuccessfully offered to a Munich brewery, set off a chain of associations in André's mind, linking the pot-bellied drinker of the drawing with the human shape Edouard had detected in the piles of tyres.

The character seemed ideal. The expression "Nunc est bibendum" came from an ode by the ancient Roman poet Horace, and had been attributed to Mark Antony, Cleopatra's ally at the naval defeat at Actium, in Greece, in the year 31 B.C. André decided to keep the reference since for him it evoked the memory of a phrase he had used while giving a talk to the Society of Civil Engineers some time before. In the course of a demonstration of the shock-absorption capacity of the inflatable tyre, he had concluded with this metaphor: "The pneumatic tyre drinks up obstacles". With this formula on the one hand, and the link between the rotund drinker and the piles of tyres on the other, André reckoned that somewhere in there he had a winner.

But how were these elements to be brought together? How could he make them work as a publicity image?

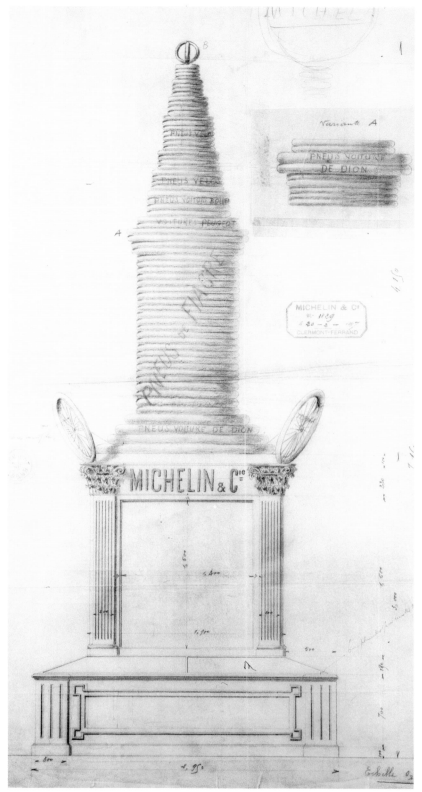

O'Galop scribbled and sketched away and came up with a little round man made of tyres, holding not a glass of beer but a mug full of nails and pieces of glass. Thus was "Nunc est bibendum" translated somewhat freely into "The tyre that drinks up obstacles". And so in April 1898 the "Michelin Man" was born in a series of posters which rapidly became famous, as famous and as familiar as the jovial character the French still call "Bibendum".

Bibendum's career as a public figure began in June when he starred as a large cardboard cut-out, on the Michelin stand at the Paris Motor Show in the Tuileries Gardens, an imposing silhouette strategically placed to impress visitors. At his feet a phonograph broadcast a series of spoken messages, popular songs and operatic airs, interspersed with slogans vaunting the merits of Michelin tyres. Visitors were hugely taken with the image of the cup of nails and shards of glass with which Bibendum quenched his inexhaustible thirst, the embodiment of a tyre "gulping down obstacles", to the extent that for a while the rubber man was also known as the "road drunkard".

Drafts for the decoration of stands, dated 1897. A drawing representing the Michelin brothers in front of the pile of tyres said to have inspired the creation of Bibendum, or the "Michelin Man".

23

At first the nail-drinker had a variety of nicknames but had not been christened officially. This came about by chance. A month later, that July, competitor Léon Théry saw André Michelin driving up in his Panhard-Levasseur to attend the Paris-Amsterdam-Paris race, and exclaimed: "Hey, here comes Bibendum!". Michelin was so amused that he decided on the spot to appropriate the name for his publicity mascot.

Delighted by his mascot's growing popularity, André Michelin decided he would take the process a stage further at the Paris Cycle Show at the Champ de Mars that December. Bibendum would of course be present, but instead of using a phonograph, his voice would be produced by a fairground barker. He appointed one of his recent recruits, a young man called Pasty, to scout for the necessary talent, someone with the stentorian tones appro-

priate to such an imposing figure as the rubber man. Unaccustomed to head-hunting missions of this kind, Pasty's first idea was to stand around the Paris markets, listening to the salesmen selling their wares. "Perfect elocution", the boss had told him. "Keen repartee... Wit without vulgarity." A tall order indeed. After a day's searching, he still had nothing to show for his efforts.

All's fair in love and war

Young Pasty was not one to be easily discouraged, however, and on reflection he decided his best chance of finding the man he wanted lay in doing the rounds of the cabarets currently flourishing following the success of Rodolphe Salis's Chat Noir cabaret. Night after night he combed the streets of Montmartre and the Latin Quarter, until one evening he found himself at the Cabaret du Ciel, at 53 boulevard de Clichy, watching an act by two comedians disguised as preachers. Just what he was looking for! And thus it was that a comedian-preacher was hired to

Page 24: *An O'Galop poster for Oury tyres, the rival firm which declared open war on Bibendum at the 1898 Paris Cycle Show.*
Above: *Reconstruction of the pile of tyres that inspired the creation of Bibendum. One of the first of the series of "Nunc est Bibendum" posters. The two puny, deflated-looking characters either side of Bibendum are caricatures of John Boyd Dunlop (left) and the head of the Continental tyre production company (right).*

lend his voice to Bibendum from 2.00 p.m. to 5.00 p.m. every day. The impersonation went so well that the massive crowd that gathered to watch and listen began to obstruct the view of the neighbouring stand; this belonged to a rival tyre company, Oury, which naturally protested, arguing that access to its stand was hindered. Since Michelin declined to do anything to discourage the crowds, Oury went onto the offensive, sparking a conflict that rapidly escalated to become the star turn of the entire Cycle Show. By way of an opening salvo, whenever Bibendum opened his mouth, Oury replied with a car horn crescendo. Despite this, the impersonator's powerful voice carried above the din. Oury added two phonographs to the sound barrage, and hired its own fairground barker to provide a

by his good friend Albert de Dion who informed the police officers: "Michelin is on his own property here, and no-one has the right to enter". Maybe it was Count de Dion's impressive cane. Maybe it was his reputation as the maker of the famous De Dion-Bouton automobiles. Whatever it was, and we shall never know for sure, the commissioner abandoned his attempt to impose silence and Bibendum was allowed to carry on entertaining the crowd.

In the closed world (as it then was) of cycling and motoring, it was clear that Bibendum had become a potent symbol. Still only a few months old, the rubber man was acquiring a strong personality, comical and boisterous, even anarchic, and in some ways primitive and boorish, in keeping with his disturbing, elephantine appearance.

The years 1894 to 1898 were decisive in the Michelin company's development. Publicity, though a vital area, was only one of its preoccupations as it sought to convince the embryonic automobile industry of the necessity of fitting its wheels with inflatable tyres. For the moment, however, it fell back on the horse-drawn carriage market. In 1896 the first hackney cab using inflatable tyres took to the streets of Paris, bringing a new market within Michelin's grasp.

Initially, Paris coach-drivers and their

rival attraction. The decibel level rose to unbearable heights. Other exhibitors, fed up with the din, joined in the commotion, most of them backing Oury and marching to the office of the organising committee president. As the recriminations multiplied, the president called the police. Assisted by four constables, a police commissioner called on André Michelin and urged him to agree a truce and end the battle of the barkers. Michelin refused, supported

employers were not keen on the prospect of having occasionally to repair punctures, particularly since they saw inflatable tyres as a luxury and a costly investment. By the end of the year, however, some 300 coaches had been fitted

Above, from left to right: The first known appearance of Bibendum in printed advertising (September 1899). Between 1901 and 1913, variations were made to the "Nunc est Bibendum" poster, accounting for the new motoring products set out on the table.
Centre: The Michelin brothers' "Eclair", 1895
Page 27, centre from left to right: The first hackney-carriage using tyres, 1896. Postcard portraying André Michelin driving an advertising hackney carriage, 1898.

with tyres of this kind, due partly to André Michelin's policy of offering generous reductions to induce reluctant operators to take up the innovation.

"We were supplying the tyres at a loss", he recalled later. "The more we sold, the more we lost on them. But that wasn't the point. The important thing was getting started and getting known. It cost us 800,000 francs the first year. But within three years every cab operator in Paris had been

won over and acknowledged the superiority -- no, more than that, the necessity -- of inflatable tyres. Above all it was the drivers who clamoured for them."

Meanwhile, as André in Paris got to grips with the cab market, Edouard and his engineers in Clermont-Ferrand had other weighty matters to think

about. The experience of the Paris-Rouen competition had convinced André of the need, as he told his brother, to "adapt the cab tyre to the automobile". At this stage, even the cab tyre was only at the experimental stage. Edouard replied that adapting it to automobile conditions was not as easy as it might appear from the comfort of the French capital.

"Cab tyres have only to cope with the made-up road surfaces of urban areas", he told André. "Tyres for automobiles will have to be able to withstand the rigours of rough ground and sharp stones. Cab tyres are used for moderate speeds, whereas motor tyres will be used at high speeds. Moreover they will be fitted to the driving wheels. This being the case, wouldn't we do better to concentrate our efforts on the horse-drawn carriage market, which is prac-

tically limitless, rather than on the automobile market which is tiny?"

"But the automobile will take over from the horse-drawn carriage as soon as it's fitted with inflatable tyres", André rejoined. "It's not yesterday's technology we should be going with, nor even with today's but with tomorrow's. And the harder the problem is to solve, the less likely it is that we'll have competition."

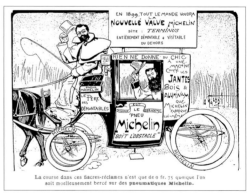

André's arguments won the day and Edouard set in train the preliminary research needed to overcome the innumerable difficulties involved in developing the new tyre. By early 1895 the programme was under way, using special wheels with steel spokes for the small Peugeot quadricycle that served for test purposes. It was almost summer by the time they achieved their first positive result. It had to be counted as an exploit rather than a victory since, positive though it may have been, it was nonetheless achieved in defeat. Competing in the Paris-Bordeaux-Paris race in their "Eclair" automobile, taking turns at the wheel, André and Edouard had finished ninth. Unfortunately the field had comprised only nine competitors. Their vehicle, a monster weighing some 2,500 pounds

performance of the Michelin vehicle in the Bordeaux race. But for once André had failed to judge the speed at which things were changing. In the event, five years were sufficient to fulfil his vision of the future. By the turn of the century inflatable tyres had become an essential component of the modern motor car. Peugeot, Delahaye, Bollée, De Dion, Panhard and even the formerly sceptical Emile Levassor were driving on Michelin's pneumatic tyres, to the merriment of Bibendum.

Having caught the mood as the vogue for cycling got under way, having been in at the birth of the automobile industry, the Michelin factory in Clermont-Ferrand had by now become a huge enterprise, a byword for innovation. In the years 1891 to 1900 sales soared from 460,000 to 6 million francs. Bibendum, at the cutting edge of Michelin's public relations, provided humorous commentary on the company's development, from Edouard's research efforts (innovation, cost reductions, improved comfort and reliability) to André's marketing battles with rival producers. Bibendum's mood was unpredictable: now jolly and obliging, he could become cheeky and cynical, then threatening and school-masterly, but always he was there, inescapable, the company's ambassador, to the public's great delight.

1900-1919: Picking up speed

Bibendum's turbulent beginnings owed a great deal to the graphic artist O'Galop, who provided much of the company's publicity material in the pre-war period. O'Galop's real name was Marius Rossillon. He was aged around 30 when he met André Michelin. He had not achieved the celebrity of his contemporary Poulbot, for example, but he was not exactly a beginner either, having drawn numerous music hall posters and two front covers for the magazine *Le Cycle*.

A regular contributor to humorous magazines such as *Le Rire* where his brother Ulysse was editor, O'Galop lent Bibendum the knockabout humour characteristic of the times and which was shared by the Michelin brothers themselves. As a student, André had been a fan of contemporary comedy singers and had even taken a course in cabaret entertainment. Edouard, who later in life acquired a reputation as an introvert, had been a live wire in his

and equipped with a vast array of repair tools, had been specially designed by Edouard and his team using Peugeot parts and a Daimler engine. It was the only vehicle in the competition using inflatable tyres. For all its many shortcomings, it succeeded in completing the 800-mile course within the stipulated limit of 100 hours. Along the way there were numerous punctures, each requiring a time-consuming repair operation, but the brothers had achieved their objective: to demonstrate that the enormous weight of a motorised vehicle could be carried on tyres containing no more than compressed air, that the pneumatic had arrived and the days of the coach and four were numbered.

For the moment, however, the motor manufacturers remained unconvinced. The winner of the race, Levassor, told the brothers: "If that's the best you can do, you can keep your sausages". André was unshaken. With characteristic self-confidence he launched a series of posters proclaiming: "In 10 years all vehicles will be fitted with pneumatic tyres". The prediction aroused widespread scepticism, if not outright mirth in view of the last-place

Above: O'Galop, alias Marius Rossillon (1867-1946), in the posture of Tartarin de Tarascon, around 1900.
Page 29: Other examples of the advertising work of O'Galop, one of the pioneers of French cartoon art. Published by l'Imagerie d'Epinal, O'Galop worked for several magazines and published several albums of his own.

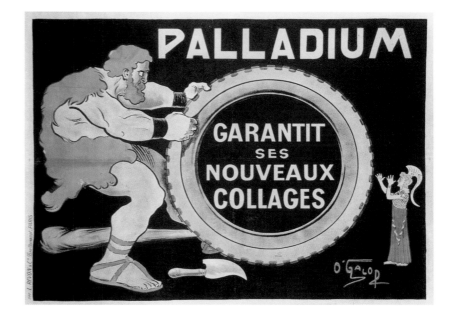

Page 30: Comic strip published
in the illustrated supplement
of the magazine Le Journal:
"The car of my friend Carbure".
O'Galop shows, with humour,
the indispensable determination
needed for driving the first
motorised tricycles, c. 1898.
Page 31: "Gribouille goes
cycling", a comic strip in the
illustrative style of Epinal,
O'Galop, 1905. Cyclist
Gribouille purchases a pair of
tyres from his friend Bibendum
but jibs at buying the matching
inner tubes. He finds some
cheaper from a competitor…
but their quality is appalling.

L'AUTO DE MON AMI CARBURE

L'autre jour je rencontre, par hasard, mon ami Gontran Carbure. « Tiens, mon vieux Galop, qu'il me fait, quelle chance! Je vais essayer mon auto à moteur conjugué : gaz, vapeur, pétrole et électricité! Viens voir ça. » Et nous voilà partis... Voici ce que j'ai vu :

GRIBOUILLE FAIT DU VÉLO, par O'GALOP.

Vous connaissez Gribouille, cet excellent, ce vieux Gribouille des familles, qui se mettait à l'eau, quand il pleuvait, pour ne pas...

...se mouiller ?... Oh ! mais, c'est qu'il a bien changé depuis ! Gribouille est devenu moderne : il pratique maintenant d'autres sports ; il fait de la bicyclette...

...mais, toujours malin, pour ne pas se fatiguer, quand ça monte, il descend, et quand ça descend, il monte.

Or, l'autre jour, il rencontre son vieux copain Bibendum : aussitôt, toujours amateur de bonne marchandise, il lui commande une...

...paire d'enveloppes et ajoute, en clignant de l'œil, d'un air malin : « Pour ce qui est de tes chambres à air rouges, mon vieux, tu ne m'auras...

...pas ; je sais un endroit où on en a pour 2 fr. 50, pas de ta marque, bien sûr, mais avec tes enveloppes, qu'est-ce que je risque ? »

Et le bougre les a eues, comme il l'avait dit, ses chambres à 2 fr. 50 la paire, métro compris, au marché aux Puces, et une fois dans les enveloppes MICHELIN, ma foi, ça avait bon air ; seulement...

...voilà, c'est bien bizarre : sitôt sur sa bécane, il roulait à plat, et il avait beau regonfler, en 2 tours de roue, il était raplat... Aussi, après 20 kilomètres de pavés, fut-il furibond ! Ses chambres n'étaient...

...plus que charpie. Et ses enveloppes, malgré leur qualité bien connue, étaient éreintées par ce métier de galérien ! En voulant économiser quelques francs, il en avait claqué 25 !

Mais Bibendum passait par là : « Eh bien, grand malin ! Cela t'apprendra à mettre dans mes bonnes enveloppes des chambres camelotes. Pourquoi pas de la paille !... ou plutôt du foin !... Et tu t'épates de rouler toujours à plat et d'être en charpie ?
« On n'attelle pas un carcan avec un pur sang. »

« Écoute un bon conseil. Monte dans tes enveloppes MICHELIN à tringles mes bonnes chambres rouges. Tu ne rouleras jamais à plat, et tu rouleras longtemps ! J'ai dit ! »
Gribouille a compris. En compagnie de Mme Gribouillette, il s'en va souriant, car tous deux ont sur leur vélo du MICHELIN dans du MICHELIN.
Et nulle panne ne trouble plus leurs amoureuses balades.

Cyclistes, suivez leur exemple, et montez sur votre machine :

dans une enveloppe Michelin à tringles,
la Chambre à air rouge Michelin.

Imp. Chassé, Sceaux. — 1601-7-1383.

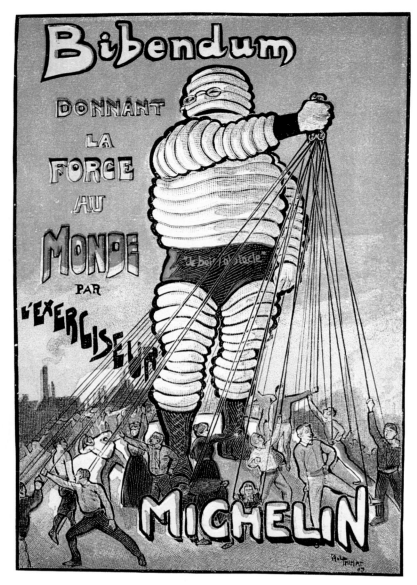

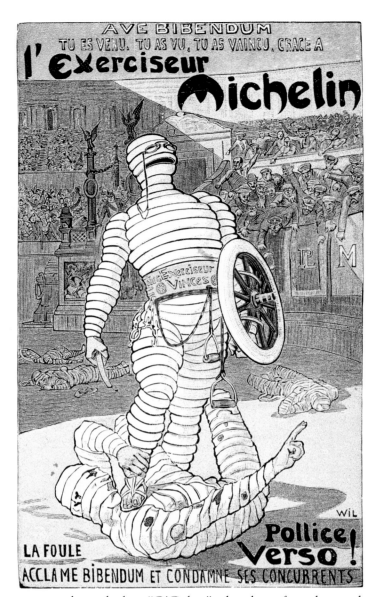

youth, punctuating his days in Bouguereau's studio with pranks and parodies of opera singers. In all likelihood there was a high degree of complicity between the graphic artist and the businessmen. The richness, consistency and longevity of their creative partnership were unusual at a time when public relations, as we now know them, were altogether a more primitive art.

The origin of the artist's full pseudonym, "O'Galop-Sonnet", is obscure. No document or independent testimony remains, but a shrewd guess would be that Rossillon chose the name because he saw his publicity work as an exercise similar to the sonnet, demanding concision, sophistication and, occasionally, the spirit of derision. Clearly he enjoyed puns and word-play. "O'Galop", the short form he used to sign his drawings, was doubtless intended to suggest to prospective clients that here was a man who could be counted on to work at speed, and that by employing him they would be on to a winner. In the race for new markets, he appeared to be saying, a product riding on O'Galop's inspiration could be counted on to finish ahead of the field.

Over the years O'Galop provided upwards of 200, maybe as many as 300, graphic designs for Michelin, most but not all of them featuring the famous rubber man. His early work focused on four main themes: technical aspects, motor racing (an activity in which Michelin was actively involved), Bibendum substituted for historical figures, and contemporary social-political references. Bibendum appeared in around 90 percent of these drawings, the remaining 10 percent being of a technical nature, relating to such matters as tyre characteristics or air pressure gauges, where his rumbustious manner might appear inappropriate.

In any event Bibendum remained true to the boisterous style of his début at the 1898 Motor Show: over-the-top, ebullient, chameleon-like. In an early newspaper advertisement of 1899 he appears, his upper half only,

perched atop a car radiator grill like the classical figures often favoured in those days. In 1901 he appears for the first time on an advertising poster, standing at a banquet table as he proposes a toast, holding aloft his glass full of nails and glass shards: "Your good health -- the Michelin tyre drinks up obstacles!". He is flanked and observed by two unhealthy-looking rivals, both grimacing with envy and discomfort, having been unable to consume the nail-glass mixture without collapsing miserably. Later the same year, for the launch of the Michelin "exerciser", O'Galop portrayed Bibendum at full length for the first time, wearing shorts and flexing his muscles like an athlete. Bibendum is visibly proud of his rippling biceps. The advertisement for Michelin's body-building device -- following the burgeoning fashion for gymnastics and other health-improving activities -- also enabled the company to portray its tyres prevailing over its rivals in a Roman arena: "Hail Bibendum! You came, you saw, you conquered".

Bibendum sees off the competition

In the beginning, Bibendum was a scrapper, a real street-fighter, since that was what the situation demanded. Advertising in those days was a great deal less regulated than it is now. Companies often had to resort to all sorts of no-holds-barred procedures simply in order to survive. An incident typical of the times occurred when the Trade and Industry Minister Alexandre Millerrand, decided to fit the bicycles of the postal service with tyres produced by Michelin's British-owned competitor Dunlop. Coming from a French minister, the decision was, to say the least, unexpected, and Michelin was quick to take up the challenge. Within days a statement was issued to the press, to be widely published under the heading "Millerrand Limited". It sharply criticised the minister's decision, stressing the British origin of Dunlop's "made in France" tyres. The importance of encouraging French industry was also highlighted in the campaign against another rival, Continental: "Continental tyres give no indication of where they

Page 32 and above: "Bibendum lends force to the world", "Hail Bibendum, you came, you saw, you conquered", "Michelin tyres resist any attack", "Michelin tyres grow stronger thanks to the exerciser": Bibendum's first appearances (1902) as a full-length figure. Promoting the exerciser at the same time as the tyre made it easier to mock the competition.
Right: Press advertisement hailing Michelin's victory in the Gordon-Bennett Cup over a course that proved a severe test for tyres (as evidenced by the poor shape of the competition).

33

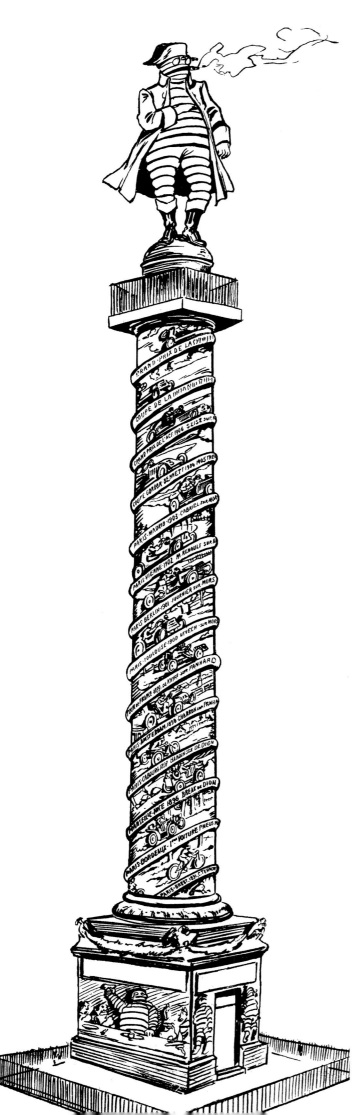

are made, or of where their head office is located. Permit us to make good their oversight: the answer is -- in Linden, near Hanover, in Germany", Michelin revealed in a brochure. A diagram in the handout, presenting Continental's Paris office as if it were linked directly by rail to Germany, was captioned: "Continental's factory in Clichy does not produce tyres: it naturalises them".

Michelin's French competitors could be equally waspish in their treatment of the market leader. Ducasble, for example, added a flyer to the O'Galop posters, answering the slogan "The Michelin tyre drinks up obstacles" with the phrase: "Yes, until it bursts". The Ducasble company produced one of those systems known as "elastic wheels", solid tyres attached to wheels in which some components, such as the spokes, hubs or rims, contained rubberised elements that were supposed to absorb shocks while at the same time avoiding the major drawback of pneumatic tyres, namely punctures. Another

firm, Roussel, whose product was similar, went straight for the jugular. Its advertisements warned darkly: "Motorists beware! The most frequent and deadly car accidents are caused by tyre blow-outs. (...) Pneumatic tyres mean death, the elastic wheel means life". Roussel's follow-up campaign, parodying a Michelin slogan that read "the pneumatic tyre gets rid of the holes in the road", proclaimed: "You got rid of the bumps, you got rid of the holes, and now we're getting rid of you". It then produced a poster portraying a dead Bibendum, over a slogan announcing: "The pneumatic tyre is slavery, the Roussel elastic wheel is freedom".

As the universally recognised symbol of the air-filled tyre, Bibendum saw no point in responding to the jibes of these small-time players and reserved his barbs for his direct competitors, the producers of other brands of pneumatic tyres. In the early drawings of O'Galop these were usually designated "tyre X" or "tyre Y" but were made

Page 34, from left to right: *The obelisk in Place Vendôme in Paris, redesigned in honour of Bibendum (1907). The Roussel elastic wheel advertising.*
From top down: *"There are 40 Immortals but only one puncture-proof tyre, it's the Ducasble automatic that drinks up obstacles but doesn't puncture". Denigrating air-filled tyres by pointing to their weak point (punctures) was the basic line of attack for producers of solid tyres. "I'm here, and I'm here to stay!" 1905 advertisement celebrating Michelin's victory in the Gordon-Bennett Cup, brochure (back and front).*

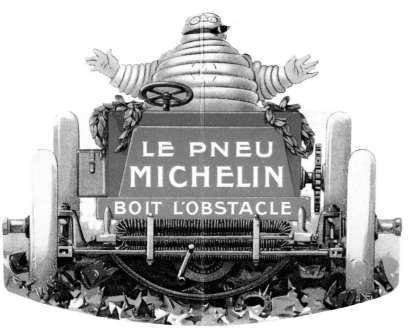

recognisable by giving their faces the features of the company chiefs, such as that of John Boyd Dunlop or the head of the Continental company. Gradually caricatures of living people were eliminated, and X and Y appeared as pitiful wretches, pale and gaunt, haggard and wan, fearful and defeated, trembling in the shadow of Bibendum's implacable might.

The demiurge

The all-powerful Bibendum began now to assume superhuman proportions. With his string of victories in the first motor races, drawing further sustenance from his international development -- factories were opened in Italy in 1906 and in the United States in 1908 -- the rubber man went from strength to strength. A postcard was issued proclaiming: "Bibendum gives strength to the world". It portrayed the company mascot manipulating the world's population as if they were so many marionettes. He became lord, king, emperor, donning the garb of the world's mightiest figures one after the other. He scorned the barriers of space and time. Now he was Napoleon overcoming the English; then he was Pharaoh, building his pyramids by the Nile, or Balthazar, the Biblical king and son of Nebuchadnezzar. And why stop at mere power? O'Galop gave his creation all the attributes of intelligence and perspicacity, presenting him in the guise of Archimedes or Descartes. Imitating the Tables of the Law drawn up in ancient Rome in the 5th century B.C., Bibendum produced his own list of commandments, not settling for 12 as the Romans did but completing a full 32. Illustrated by O'Galop, these aimed to provide a guide to good driving and the proper

maintenance of pneumatic tyres, as for example: "Thou shalt take the turn in the road with all due precaution, like a good family man", or: "Thou shalt refrain from nipping the inner tube by fitting it carelessly".

Transposing with ease from one symbol to another, Bibendum became in turn the Heracles of the tyre, the Themis of the road, while retaining human feelings as the protagonists of Greek and Latin mythology did 2,000 years ago. Mythological references came in useful when looking for new names to designate the company's latest products.

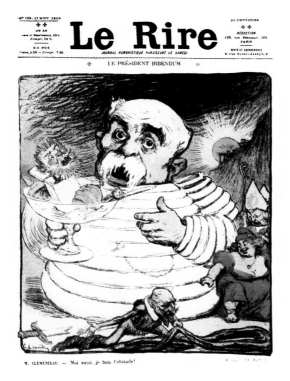

M. CLEMENCEAU. — Moi aussi, je bois l'obstacle!

Thus Michelin produced the "Paradise" repair kit, in which you were as likely as not to find bolts dubbed "Dalila" or "Damocles". More and more the rubber man assumed the role of the motorist's guardian angel, a thoughtful pedagogue, as immediately popular as he had previously been mischievous. Of all the many creations of advertising, Bibendum is perhaps the only one to have developed such a strong yet complex personality, blowing hot and cold in his social attitudes, displaying insolence one moment, affability the next, by turn pitiless or indulgent.

Represented at the wheel of a car, Bibendum resembled the typical motorist of the time, wrapped in the sheepskin coat essential for driving in uncovered vehicles. His temperament was an idealised reflection of the

Humourists from the turn of the century onwards turned to Bibendum as a means of caricaturing politicians in difficulty. In 1906, French minister Georges Clemenceau appeared on the front cover of a magazine with this slogan: "I too drink up obstacles". Popularity as seen by O'Galop, 1906.

perceived temperament of the contemporary motorist, the intrepid explorer in his "horseless" carriage setting off on an expedition. His accessories -- goggles and cigar -- were the official insignia of his membership of that privileged minority who enjoyed the means and the leisure to take up motoring. Imperceptibly he began to display the signs of weakness attributed to the bourgeoisie of the time, at least as seen by cartoonists. Or so one would deduce from a drawing by O'Galop portraying the Michelin mascot as a ladies' man, surrounded by soubrettes.

The price of tyres in the 1890s was exorbitant, even bicycle tyres, which in 1892 cost 165 francs a pair -- this at a time when a workman's average wage was of the order of six francs a day. Even allowing for a sharp fall in the price, down by around 50 percent within two years, a tyre remained a luxury product, often displayed as such in white crêpe paper. This would perhaps explain why Bibendum always appeared in white, though the tyres of the period were a uniform grey. But a simpler and more obvious explanation would be that white made the rubber man more visible and easier to read.

Asked what made a poster effective, O'Galop replied: "The most important quality is the way it *expresses* its meaning. What I mean is, for want of a simpler word, that it must very rapidly and clearly convey what the manufacturer has asked the artist to convey: the message that such and such a product has such and such advantages. That has to be clear in the drawing, or at the very least in the text and, in the latter case, the drawing has to draw attention to the text.

"Which leads me to the second quality, almost -- but only almost -- as important as the first: visibility. The poster absolutely must attract attention. Once it has done that, it has achieved its objective. The product has been presented; it is up to the product to do the rest."

As an expression of the advertiser's creed, O'Galop's dictum could hardly be bettered even today.

Deutsche Michelin-Pneumatik A.G.
MAINZERLANDSTRASSE 116   FRANKFURT A. MAIN

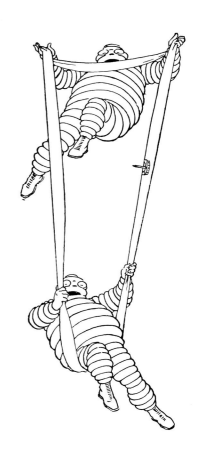

Page 38, top: *"I have it. My real belt of strength", German postcard of 1907 vaunting the merits of the Michelin anti-skid tyre.*
Page 38, bottom: *Allusion to the many victories gained by Michelin in motor racing, 1904 postcard.*
From left to right and from top down: *"Soldiers, from the summit of this pyramid, more than 40 victories look down on you" -- a reference to words spoken by Napoleon Bonaparte to his troops during the Egyptian campaign (1905). Cover of the magazine* Il Pneumatico Michelin *drawn by Carlo Biscaretti di Ruffia, 1910. One of the educational components of the campaign: "Weight is the enemy! In a motorcar, a five percent increase in weight means a 14 percent increase in wear and tear on tyres" (German advertisement, 1905).*
Page 40: *O'Galop poster published in 1905, marking the creation in Britain of the Michelin Tyre Co. Ltd.*

Chapter 3
A talent
for publicity

GUIDE MICHELIN

Offert

gracieusement

aux

Chauffeurs

ÉDITION 1900

"Our guiding principle was absolutely straightforward: combine efficacy with pleasure." André Michelin's philosophy of advertising could thus be summed up in a phrase of Biblical simplicity. The essential modernity of his approach, clearly looking ahead to the dawning of the 20th century, contrasted sharply with the prevailing norms in advertising, where illustrations were rare and texts tended to be long-winded, monotonous and off-putting. The development of colour printing on the other hand meant that poster advertising was about to take off as never before. Some of France's most eminent artists of the 1890s, such as Chéret, Toulouse-Lautrec and Mucha, devoted their talents to this new medium, with the result that the end product was often more esthetically pleasing than commercially effective. A clear example of this was the "chérettes" -- named after the artist Chéret -- which, whether used to advertise cough pastilles, hair-lotion or a night out at the ball, appeared interchangeable.

One of Michelin's early advertising exploits, in the days following the Paris-Rouen race, was a vivid demonstration of the air-filled tyre's superiority by means of a fairground roundabout. At the 1895 Paris Cycle Show, held in the Industry Pavilion on the Champs-Elysées, a roundabout was set up with two chairs, one fitted with pneumatic tyres and the other using wheels with a steel band around the rim. The chairs were wheeled round a circular track along which a variety of bumps and obstructions had been placed. The passenger who opted for the chair with the steel-rimmed wheels was given a rough ride "worthy of the Inquisition", André Michelin affirmed. The passenger who rode on air-filled tyres by contrast enjoyed a comfortable, trouble-free journey. The demonstration had its comic side, and large crowds gathered around the Michelin stand to enjoy the spectacle. Part of the fun was observing the dainty young women riders whose skirts would billow in the wind, offering enticing glimpses of their frilly underclothes. Having noted this unintended bonus, André arranged for a young beauty to be present during the official visit to the stand by Félix Faure, the French president well-known for his weakness for the fair sex. Faure was more than happy to stop off at the stand and interested enough to stay until the end of the demonstration.

The story of "Michelin's roundabout" is more than an amusing anecdote. It clearly illustrates the principle underlying the company's advertising strategy. This was to win over the public by inducing it to try out the product, by whatever means, so that it could compare it with that of rival producers. The compare-and-contrast principle was the reason why André Michelin took part in so many of the earliest motor races, often taking the wheel himself: the object was to demonstrate the superiority of the air-filled tyre over solid tyres. Having done this by winning almost all the major races of the time (the Paris-Marseilles-Paris in 1896, the Paris-Amsterdam-Paris in 1898, the Tour de France in 1899 and many others), André announced that the company would no longer take part in such events in order to "eliminate needless expenditure" and to concentrate on "producing the best tyre for the lowest possible cost".

Presenting another innovation, André Michelin wrote, without undue modesty: "This publication was born with the century, and will last just as long". History has borne out André's prediction, made in the preface to the first edition of the *Michelin Guide*, the 35,000 copies of which were issued free by Michelin agents. The pocket-sized guide with the red cover

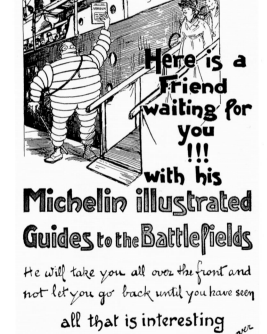

aimed to provide motorists with "all the information necessary when driving around France to find supplies and repairs for your automobile, and food and overnight accommodation for yourself". Inevitably the information would be incomplete in this inaugural edition, André admitted, but this could be remedied: he invited motorists to send in details of their experiences when travelling around the country. "Without our readers we can do nothing; with them we can do everything", he wrote. The system of awarding stars was introduced, but only to hotels, not yet to restaurants. The publisher warned that subsequent editions would omit the names of hotels where "the

Page 42: *First edition of the Michelin Guide.*
Revised every year since its inception in 1900, the guide was issued free to motorists until 1920.
Right: *British advertisement for Michelin guides to the battlefields, a collection comprising several dozen titles published in English and French between 1917 and 1928.*

food, rooms, toilets or service" were found to be wanting. There were no grounds as yet for hoteliers to start quaking in their boots -- in 1900 the number of cars in France totalled 2 897 precisely -- but that would change. As the cost of a "horseless carriage" fell and its reliability increased, within a few years the guide, now on sale in bookshops, began to be considered a quality product, and it became a matter of prestige to be listed in its pages.

The *Michelin Guide* (with Bibendum on the back cover of the 1901 edition, in a quarter-page advertisement for the exerciser) was the first move towards what many manufacturers saw as a necessary step: creating a package of services for the motorist at the same time as promoting their products. The object was to help the motorist find his way around the country. To this effect, Michelin set up a route information service (1908), began publishing road-maps (1910) and issued regional guides (1926), the precursors of the green guides which were to become an essential accessory for generations of migrating holiday-makers. In time, initiatives such as these -- going well beyond what would normally be expected of a tyre manufacturer -- served to associate the brand name in the public mind with motoring activities of every kind, making Michelin a quasi-official partner in developing the road system and improving transport and tourism infrastructures.

In 1901 André Michelin began placing advertisements in the press on fixed dates, a procedure that ran counter to general practice at the time. Advertising in those days displayed a total lack of co-ordination and continuity. No manufacturer had previously considered taking out space in the press to provide its own slant on what was happening within the company. The Michelin advertisements provided virtually the first example of a sustained, conscious publicity campaign conducted over a period of time.

The weekly bulletin was timed to appear on Mondays, the day of the week when Michelin's target readers were likely to be most assiduous in their newspaper reading, in order to keep up with the races and other sports events of the weekend. The first advertisement, headed "Michelin Mondays", appeared on March 11 in *L'Auto-Vélo*, later shortened to *L'Auto*, founded by the noted racing cyclist Henri Desgranges, who already owned the "Vel' d'Hiv" velodrome in the southwest of Paris, and who two years later, in 1903, was to initiate the Tour de France cycle race. The bulletin varied widely in its subject-matter, ranging from disputes with the administration to advice on fitting an inner tube, from presenting a new product to tips on how to pass the driving test. Over the months and years it provided a broad panorama

BRITISH ISLES   ALPES ᴇᴛ RHIN   LES PAYS DU SOLEIL   ESPAÑA Y PORTUGAL   DEUTSCHLAND

CE
QUE
MICHELIN
A FAIT POUR
Le TOURISME

GUIDES MICHELIN

BUREAUX DE TOURISME

PLAQUES INDICATRICES

CARTES MICHELIN

Page 44, from top down: "Michelin maps", 1912 leaflet with the key to symbols on Michelin
maps published from 1910 onwards. "The route information service", a 1923 poster.
Above: "What Michelin has done for tourism", 1912 leaflet, indicating that the company pub-
lishes guides to foreign countries. From 1904 Michelin began publishing its red guides for countries where its products were sold.

of every possible issue relating to motoring. Every week, over the title, a drawing would attract the eye of the reader, featuring Bibendum in a variety of situations, for example as an angel smiling down from a cloud, or as an accordionist playing for a beautiful Italian woman. One week he appears as a Roman emperor being greeted by Louis XIV, the next week he appears arm-in-arm with the President of the French Republic, Armand Fallières. As the influence of the Michelin bulletin grew, similar features were introduced by rival tyre producers Continental and Dunlop and by the motor companies De Dion, Peu-

geot and Delahaye. None of them managed to maintain the consistency of the "Michelin Mondays", which were discontinued only with the outbreak of the first World War. The last Michelin bulletin, number 690, appeared on July 27, 1914, ending an unbroken run of 13 years.

A team of writers was appointed to compile and edit the bulletin, which provided a lively digest of comment and information. Viewed as a long-term investment, it embodied André Michelin's deep-seated belief that publicity was one of those activities which had to be done properly or not at all. From 1911 onwards the same team of

writers produced another original form of advertising, an "illustrated play". The company bought space on the cover of *L'Illustration théâtrale*, a supplement to the weekly magazine *L'Illustration* devoted to theatre which had never previously carried advertising. It devised a sketch, broadly in keeping with the rest of the supplement, in which the various incidents that tend to arise over the lifetime of a tyre were presented in dramatic form. For example, one of them, entitled "The Semi-virgins", dealt with the porosity of used inner tubes; another, entitled "To Serve", highlighted the tyre's long-lasting qualities. Bibendum played a cameo role in these sketches, often providing a humorous counterpoint. This formula too was brought to an end by the war, the last sketch appearing on July 25, 1914.

Michelin's tourist office, introduced in 1908, was perhaps the most clearcut example of the company's determination to be seen as a public service. Its task was to provide motorists, on request, with the information needed to get from A to B in the shortest possible time. A service of this kind might appear unnecessary nowadays, but in those pioneering days it was essential. The service was "free, like education, and bound to become just as obligatory (...) by becoming indispensable", Michelin announced in an advertisement, not without good reason. The road network in the early 1900s was in poor shape, the age of the horse-drawn coach having given way to the age of the railway, so that road-users were less familiar with the highways and byways of their own country than they were with the exotic names of trans-continental steam-trains such as the Orient Express or the Trans-Siberian. The new generation of road-users, at the steering wheels of their motorcars, found themselves driving around in circles in the dust raised by their vehicles, while crowds of bemused villagers, who had never in their lives seen wheeled contraptions capable of reaching such dizzying speeds, looked on in wonderment.

The number of vehicles in France remained small: just 12,000 in 1906. In that first year, barely 100 requests for

Page 46: Publication of the "red guides" and road maps, creation of a route information service and the setting-up of road signs: Michelin's various initiatives to encourage tourism were a form of indirect promotion of the company's tyres.
From left to right: *Advertising menu designed by Ernest Montaut (1905).*
Programme cover by E. L. Cousyn (1913).

Cot, Cot..... Codek !

La Centième de Michelin

La centième ! Vous pensez peut-être : " Ami
Bibendum, pourquoi tant de réclame ? A bon
vin, point d'enseigne ! "

Lisez cette petite histoire que je tiens des
paysans de mon village :

Quand une cane a pondu un œuf, que fait-elle ?
Elle ne dit rien et retourne à sa mare.

Quand une poule a pondu un œuf, que fait-
elle ? Elle se dresse sur le plus haut perchoir
et chante : Cot, Cot, Codek! Cot, Cot, Codek !
et encore Cot, Cot, Codek ! et toujours Cot, Cot, Codek !

Résultat : Tout le monde demande des œufs de poule, personne ne demande des œufs de cane.
Vous me direz que les œufs de poule sont meilleurs. Sans doute. Mais encore faut-il qu'on le sache, —
et qu'on sache surtout qu'ils sont pondus.

Moi aussi, je chante, Cot, Cot, Codek ! afin que nul n'ignore que Michelin, mon père,
fabrique des pneus... et que ces pneus sont les meilleurs du monde.

route information were received. By the 1920s, however, numbers began picking up and the office had to take on as many as 80 employees to provide the average 5,000 itineraries requested each month. The requests were received by post or by telephone and forwarded to a processing centre which would give them a number in order for them to be dealt with by a "route specialist". These specialists, allocated tasks by categories such as the nature of the journey (excursions, short journeys or grand tours) or geographical area (France, Central Europe, Northern Europe, Mediterranean) were able to draw on a vast array of maps plus the office's own documentary resources. These included many itineraries broken down into short stretches with a detailed account of their particulars: the towns and villages along the way, the state of the road, sights to be seen... The files were constantly updated with information provided by the inspectors of the Michelin Guides department in a natural system of feedback between the company and its clientele.

The office, by then a mine of valuable information, changed its name and became the route information service. Its emblem portrayed Bibendum struggling under a mountain of documents. With car sales increasing by 300 percent during the 1920s, the service's growing reputation reflected considerable credit on the company. The rapidity with which requests for information were met (within a maximum of 48 hours) and the comprehensiveness of the information provided (as many as 100 typed pages) created indirect publicity that was all the more effective in that it dealt with every aspect of the motorist's concerns without regard to the particular brand of tyre that he used. A climate of confidence was established with travellers who very often would write in with their impressions, providing a store of information that could then be used to correct and update the service's files. In this way the company name acquired a considerable fund of sympathy and credibility.

In all this Bibendum gradually assumed the role of the motorist's guardian angel. There was no question, however, of his neglecting his original role of public clown, particularly in the carnivals that flourished at the turn of the century, where his exuberance and irreverence contributed to the general mood of catharsis and excess. "There are those who find Bibendum's entertaining antics rather too much of a good thing", wrote one chronicler. "Our illustrious rubber man has decided to take his leave of the motor shows and exhibitions and parade his charming undulations on the public highway.

At the Lent carnival, the people of Paris rejoiced at his arrival since, as is well known, the mere sight of him is sufficient to fill the onlooker with merriment. A 12-foot-tall Bibendum towered down from his float, while in his shadow two smaller Michelin Men besported themselves with great brio..."

Escorted by a group of folk dancers from Clermont-Fer-

![ENTREZ! VENEZ SIGNER APRÈS LE Président de la République Française LA PÉTITION POUR LE Numérotage des Routes dont la Maison MICHELIN a pris l'initiative]

rand in the Auvergne region, who handed out flowers and showered confetti, Bibendum also paraded his talents at the Nice carnival, perched on a float amid a swathe of nails and shards of glass. A colossal figure with his arms

extended, he struck a heroic pose resembling those emperors of history bestowing their favours on a grateful people. In those days of the Belle Epoque, popular carnivals, financed by corporations, guilds and small tradesmen, became a favoured means for major enterprises to reach the general public. Thus figures of carnival mythology would stand alongside mascots and emblems of brands such as Michelin or the Le Printemps department store, in spectacular cavalcades that blended tradition and the glories of modern industry.

Every road needs a number

Finding your way around an unknown region in the first decade of the 20th century, when there were few cars and even fewer road signs, required skills beyond the reach of the common mortal. Roads were classified in four categories: national, departmental, regular traffic and local traffic. The system of indicating distances appeared to be totally random. "There is a total lack of method", the magazine *La Vie automobile* tut-tutted. Size, shape, markings -- everything was a complete jumble. Often the milestones bore no marking at all, or referred to some administrative benchmark unknown to the passing motorist and were decipherable only to local engineers. "Something is needed to revolutionise automobile tourism", one of the "Michelin Mondays" commented. "We suggest that all roads be given a number that is indicated on road-maps and on the roads themselves."

It was at the 1912 Paris Air Show, during the inauguration by President Armand Fallières on October 26, that André Michelin launched a nationwide petition demanding that French roads be systematically numbered. The president was among the first signatories. Seizing the opportunity provided by this unexpected patronage, the organisers issued a poster bordered with the colours of the French flag and reproducing a photograph of Fallières signing the petition,

Alongside his publicity campaigns in the printed media, the Michelin mascot featured, from the outset, as a large-scale presence on carnival floats and exhibition stands.
Left and bottom: Bibendum at the Nice Carnival, 1908-10.
Right: At the Seville Carnival (Spain), in 1930.
Opposite: Displaying a high degree of sophistication, the Michelin carnival floats and exhibition stands of the period drew on the talents of a large number of decorators.
Pages 52-53: Bibendum in all his splendour at the Nice Carnival (1908-10).

watched by several Bibendums perched on a platform in the background. The poster urged the public to follow the president's example and sign the petition. Within a month 200,000 signatures had been added, to be presented with great ceremony to the Public Works ministry. On March 17, 1913 Minister Jean Dupuy signed the decree ordering that a system of road-numbering be established.

Following this successful exercise in lobbying, André embarked on a series of campaigns of an overtly more political nature, in which he sought to impress his views on the public authorities. While Bibendum continued his clowning in the "Michelin Mondays", the Michelin brothers were growing increasingly concerned by the threat of war. In Februry 1912 the brothers, both aviation enthusiasts, issued a brochure entitled *Our Future is in the Air*, of which more than a million copies were printed. Their tone of voice was grave; this had nothing to do with motoring, recreational or otherwise: "The empire of the air is there for the taking. Whoever gains supremacy in the air compa-

force was taken up. By the time the armistice was declared four years later, Michelin's factories had turned out 1,884 warplanes.

After the war, Michelin suddenly decided to stop advertising in the printed press. This was a deliberate choice following an attempt by the Havas agency to secure a monopoly by bringing all the significant advertising outlets in the media under its control. The strategy of power-hungry Havas president Léon Rénier aroused concern at government level, with the police department warning in a report: "The danger of placing control of advertising in the French press in the hands of just one man should be quite clear". Exercising his power over newspaper advertising with the utmost ruthlessness, Rénier laid down the following terms: advertisers would have to accept his conditions or simply do without access to the printed media. André Michelin was not going to have any of this. Among the projects he abandoned was the resumption of the "Michelin Mondays".

rable to Britain's supremacy over the seas will have nothing to fear from invasion". For the moment, however, the warning fell on deaf ears. War was declared on August 3, 1914, but it was not until November 11 that Michelin's offer to place its factories and its technical expertise at the disposition of the state to build an air

He decided instead to focus on direct mail shots, both in France and in other countries where the firm had retail outlets. Mailing lists of motorists drawn up before the war were rapidly updated and thousands of handbills and brochures in several languages were sent out from the Paris office. Bibendum was everywhere. Cigar in hand,

he would vaunt the merits of a new tyre or of the "puncture warning system", an ingenious cartridge device fitted to the rim of the wheel, or urge motorists to avail themselves of the route information service. A typical example was the four-page leaflet setting out the advantages of the "cable" tyre -- a tyre using two layers of parallel cord fabrics instead of the classic rubberised-canvas sheets placed at right-angles to each other. In November 1922, some 500,000 copies of this prospectus, translated into several languages, were sent out, not counting the

headache, and mailing costs sky-rocketed. Moreover, to achieve any significant inroads into the market, there was no real alternative to the printed press, the only way of reaching the general public.

In the circumstances it can hardly have been by chance that Havas, in 1923, contacted Michelin with a view to reopening talks. The two companies were complementary; they could hardly go on ignoring each other. Havas harboured a sneaking fear that Michelin, one of the country's leading industrialists and formerly

French-language edition. Of these, 215,000 copies went to Britain, 117,000 copies to Spain, 40,000 to the Netherlands, 33,000 to Sweden, 26,000 to Portugal, 20,000 to Germany and 18,000 to Denmark.

Deprived of his usual audience of newspaper readers, Bibendum was forced to vent his frustrations by means of permanent appearances in the company's mail. This was the time when Michelin began to use the superb Bibendum alphabet, featuring the rubber man playing around within the capital letters at the head of each paragraph. He would be found reclining within the curve of the letter C, swinging from the crossbar of the H, leaning against the leg of the K, or supporting the lower bar of the Z. The Michelin logo printed on envelopes featured a ballet of Bibendums dancing among the eight letters which spelt the company's name.

The automobile market expanded considerably over the ensuing years. While sales remained well below the mass-production levels achieved by Ford in the United States, the number of vehicles owned in Europe continued to rise, totalling around 500,000 in France alone. For Michelin, maintaining customer lists became an increasing

a major advertiser, might carry on indefinitely pursuing its development without recourse to the printed media. And that this might give ideas to other advertisers.

The dubious advertising practices of the period -- the lack of information about payment to agents, the incompetence, the mediocrity and the charlatanism of many of its practitioners -- meant that for many the profession was little more than "a school for lies, slander, impudence and gossip", to quote the literary weekly *Candide*. Michelin, however, could not afford to go on ignoring the power of the press, particularly as it was preparing a major survey into the budgetary aspects of motoring, in a bid to determine how much motorists spent on purchasing and maintaining their vehicles. And so, overcoming their mutual antagonism, Michelin and Havas struck a deal: the agency would allow *Le Petit Parisien* to carry out the survey, free of charge, with the support of other newspapers that were bound contractually to Havas. The operation was a success, and Michelin resumed its collaboration with the press. Between May 1924 and May 1925 it ran an extensive promotional campaign in the five major Paris dailies (not to mention a wide range of regional and local publications, in all a total of 253 titles), publishing a series of articles on the theme "Developing the use of the motor

Pre-1914 and 1920s logo-lettering used in the company's letterhead and envelopes.
Pages 56-57: Alphabet (1919).

11.023

11.024

11.025

11.026

11.027

11.028

11.029

11.030

11.031

11.032

11.033

11.034

11.035

11.036

11.037

11.038

11.039

11.040

11.041

11.042

11.043

11.044

11.045

11.046

11.047

11.048

car" and discussing the advantages of motor transport by means of economic and statistical analysis.

"The motor car makes life easier for women, particularly in the countryside", was the conclusion of one article. "It is easier to learn to drive a car than to learn to ride a horse", another argued. "The motor car costs between three and ten times less to run than a horse", another concluded, backing up its argument with an array of figures: "Farmers and businessmen who use horses, have you stopped to work out how much they cost to feed? A 10 horse-power motor car which consumes nine litres of petrol and a third of a litre of oil per 100 kilometres costs 20 francs at current prices, i.e. 20 centimes per kilometre.

A horse that works every day covers at most 6,000 kilometres per year. Feeding it will cost 3,600 francs. A motor car will cover the same distance for 1,200 francs, i.e. three times less. (...) In addition to fuel and oil, a motor car requires tyres for its wheels. But then a horse needs horseshoes for its hooves. We will compare these costs in our next issue". Inevitably the following article found that expenditure on tyres worked out at much less than the cost of horse-shoes: "10 francs a month less for a five or six horse-power vehicle using the latest design of large tyre".

Car ownership was still extremely limited and the impact of the Michelin campaign was wide-ranging, providing would-be car owners with the detailed arguments they needed to take the plunge. Oddly enough, the campaign "does not seek to promote Michelin in particular, nor even to promote tyres as a whole", one journalist observed. "This is in fact educational, documented public-

ity in favour of the motor car. You might well argue that the more motor cars are sold, the greater will be the demand for tyres. It must nevertheless be admitted that this is a bold notion, launching an educational campaign on behalf of the motor car in order to develop sales of tyres and thus to bring benefit to Michelin. Never let it be said that French industry and French businessmen are incapable of taking a long-term outlook."

The campaign -- in which Bibendum featured prominently -- cost Michelin four million francs, a fortune at the time and a boon for the Havas agency, who contacted André Michelin to say that they would like to pay "a courtesy visit". The prospect was more than he could stomach.

"Tell them I won't see them", he said. "They disgust me." His revulsion was widely shared by the media, which were pressing, still unsuccessfully, for greater openness and a code of proper practice in the advertising industry.

Bibendum and the "pigs campaign"

However disillusioned he might have felt with some members of the profession, André was nonetheless one of its most adept practitioners, and in the spring of 1924 he launched a master-stroke bordering on genius. The "pigs campaign" exemplified that subtle blend of method and fantasy that had become the Michelin brothers' trademark. Its objective was to persuade the Paris public transport authority to fit its buses with air-filled tyres and get rid of

"People of Paris! An outrage! Pigs on air-filled tyres! You on solid tyres! Demand equal treatment!" Postcards distributed during the famous "pigs campaign", orchestrated by André Michelin in 1924 to induce the Paris bus company to fit its vehicles with pneumatic tyres.

the solid tyres it had insisted on maintaining until then. And so one morning in June the commuters of Paris awoke to find the city streets dotted with thousands of posters, of all shapes and sizes, in which they were shown to be getting a raw deal compared with pigs. On one side of the poster, passengers were shown boarding a bus mounted on solid tyres; the other half showed a troop of pigs boarding a lorry fitted with pneumatic tyres. The poster proclaimed: "People of Paris! This is an outrage! Pigs travel on air-filled tyres, while you have to bounce along on solid tyres. Demand equal treatment!".

The general public found the posters hilarious. The campaign, which had been carefully prepared in great

you're fed up with travelling on Paris buses with their solid tyres and fancy a gentler ride, all you need to do is get yourself carted off by the police", one card read. Another noted: "Even pumps get a better ride than bus passengers".

The following Sunday was the day when the people of Paris traditionally turned out in the Bois de Boulogne, the woody park in the west of the city, to watch the well-to-do ride past in their horse-drawn carriages to the Longchamp racecourse for the annual Grand Prix. The event, a parade of elegant ladies in their expensive clothes and extravagant hats, was

Ce " panier à salade " roule sur pneus et non sur pleins,
parce que c'est plus économique.
Quand, las de souffrir en autobus sur bandages pleins, les Parisiens voudront enfin connaître un transport en commun confortable, ils auront toujours la ressource de se faire coffrer.
1-4.596-6-2420 - R. C. 147.754, SEINE
La collection est envoyée gratuitement sur demande adressée à
MICHELIN, 97, *Boulevard Pereire* - PARIS (XVIIᵉ)

Elle aussi, on "LA" transporte sur pneus et non sur pleins,
parce que c'est plus économique.
parce que cela fait moins de tapage dans la rue.
Si les autobus roulent encore sur bandages pleins, c'est donc que l'argent des Parisiens n'a pas d'odeur et que leur repos est chose négligeable ?
1-4.596-6 2420 - R. C. 147.754, SEINE
La collection est envoyée gratuitement sur demande adressée à
MICHELIN, 97, *Boulevard Pereire* - PARIS (XVIIᵉ)

detail, benefited from the effect of surprise in achieving its objective. Poster sites had been chosen individually, as close as possible to bus termini. Some hoardings, such as the one rented at the Porte de Champerret, were massive, covering more than 600 square feet, and attracted large crowds of amused motorists and passers-by. Smaller stickers were also posted by the roadside and some shopkeepers, entering into the irreverent spirit of things, volunteered to place them free in their shop windows. At the same time, hundreds of office-workers organised petitions in favour of pneumatic tyres on buses and had them delivered to the town hall, in some cases accompanied by a legal summons. A series of postcards was printed, several thousands of copies at a time, presenting variations on the original poster, showing other vehicles that ran on air-filled tyres, ranging from wine and coal lorries to police Black Marias and the mobile pumps used for emptying septic tanks. "If

one of the highlights of the year, a spectacle much appreciated at a time when France had yet to throw off the burden -- not just financial and material but also psychological -- of the First World War. Suddenly, breaking into the long cortege of coaches with their elegant occupants, a fleet of lorries burst on the scene, swerving into the main avenue to the cheers of the crowd. On the side of the lorries was a poster of the septic pump vehicle on rubber tyres, an image which, amidst the elegance of the occasion, the spectators found particularly droll. Driving the leading lorry was 71-year-old André Michelin, his hair and beard streaming in the wind, his eyes sparkling behind his pince-nez glasses. When the police intervened to order a halt to the procession of lorries, it was André who with relish jumped from his cab to negotiate with the commanding officer and to persuade him to allow them to continue on their way.

At this point André might have settled for having made his point in this dramatic fashion, but he was not finished yet. The concluding stage of the operation took place a few days later at one of Paris's most symbolic landmarks: the Place de la Concorde, opposite the French parliament, or National Assembly. A specially rented bus drew up on the square in front of a lorry, also specially hired for the occasion, full to the brim with pigs. The bus passengers -- Michelin employees -- dismounted and staged a mock attack on the lorry, dragging the pigs out into the road to take their places in the truck. Passing motorists and pedestrians could hardly believe their eyes. Drivers stopped to watch, and within minutes the square was completely snarled up amid the chaos and cacophony of honking car horns, shouting bystanders and shrieking pigs. A quick phone call ensured that newsreel cameramen were rapidly on the scene to capture the surreal moment for posterity as Michelin's men sat in the seats formerly occupied by the pigs. Within months the urban transport authority had reversed its decision to continue using solid tyres.

News of the pigs campaign was carried far and wide by newsreel and press reports, not just at home but also abroad, notably to Britain where it was considered a typical piece of French farce. It indeed needed the Parisians' cheek and rebellious spirit to dream up, let alone carry off, a publicity stunt of this kind.

Long afterwards the planning and execution of the pigs campaign was taken by the professional advertising media as a case study, a model of its kind. Even now it is a striking example of the mobilising of resources to optimal effect, employing three forms of poster advertising (roadside posting, fly posting, unofficial and mobile posting) allied to a non-media campaign involving postcards, a form of lobbying by means of a petition, and a crowning event, or what would nowadays be described as a happening, guaranteed to attract maximum press coverage. Even today few campaigns have so impressed by their comprehensive nature. Historians of French advertising have generally set the date of the first major publicity event as 1925, the year that André Citroën, during the International Decorative Arts Exhibition, succeeded in having his company's name emblazoned in lights on the Eiffel Tower. However, the pigs campaign of the previous year has been largely

Publicity vehicles in the late 1920s. Top and centre: *Some of the vehicles had loudspeakers that could address passers-by. The Bibendum figure could be made to move from inside the vehicle by means of levers.*
Bottom: *This Renault 6CV on heavy tyres drove around Paris during the 1929 Motor Show.*
Page 61, from top down: *Preparations for a publicity parade in Japan, around 1928. Publicity parade in Argentina, 1923.*

overlooked as an example of coherence and wit going well beyond the Citroën achievement which, apart from displaying the force of conviction needed to obtain the approval of the public authorities, was essentially banal.

André Michelin's contribution to dragging French advertisers out of their torpor in the 1920s was considerable. Stereotypes and clichés continued to prevail in many areas, but there was also, here and there, a new desire to speak honestly and openly, to use more subtle means in which evocation was more important that mere representation, giving rise to original forms of advertising. "New and striking kinds of poster and media advertising appeared which displayed an intimate understanding of what was being sold", enthused Roger-Louis Dupuy in the magazine *Vendre*. Dupuy, a former engineer who founded his own agency, went on to become one of the godfathers of French advertising. Citing such poster designers as Cas-

sandre and Loupot, Dupuy singled out Michelin as a precurser of modern advertising at a time when the norm was still for "vain affirmations and brash superlatives, as if the product in question was the only one of its kind in the world".

The only one in the world... Michelin rigorously avoided such naive assertions, particularly in foreign markets, and gave due consideration to the keen competition provided by the US firm Goodyear and Britain's Dunlop. The company strove tirelessly to find spectacular new ways of establishing the superiority of its product, for example launching a campaign aimed at highlighting the advantages of the latest technological development, the low-pressure tyre. This product, dubbed the "Comfort", was presented by a group of stuntmen who travelled from town to town performing the most amazing acrobatics to demonstrate that the tyre stayed within the rim even in the most extreme conditions. At the same time, this determination to vaunt the merits of the pneumatic tyre took on even greater proportions. The archetype in the 1920s

From top down: The Michelin float at the 1911 Nice Carnival conveyed a protest by the company against the government's refusal to provide funds for the construction of military aircraft. Hence an aircraft without wings landing on top of a house. "63 percent of the tyres on vehicles displayed at the Grand Palais on the Champs-Elysées are Michelin tyres" -- 1912 leaflet. Page 63, from top down: Bibendum as a car-radiator stopper, 1922. Advertising stamps issued in 1923. British stand, around 1927.

was the Coca Cola company, whose product and red-and-white colours were spreading around the globe at a phenomenal rate. Perhaps it was the influence of American publicity practices, perhaps there were other reasons, but whatever the cause, it was at this point that André Michelin, emulating Coca Cola president Robert Woodruff who said humanity could be divided into two categories, "those who drink Coca Cola and those who are going to drink Coca Cola", decided that Bibendum had to become a permanent fixture in the daily life of his clients.

The company's policy between 1927 and 1930 was aimed at publishing the image of the rubber man so widely that he would accompany the motorist from the time he got up in the morning to when he went to bed at night. Wherever he looked he would find Bibendum: on his

breakfast bowl, on his knife, fork and spoon, on his butter dish, on his bar of chocolate; on his soap and on his bottle of perfume. At work he would find the company's symbol on his ink-well or on his pen; in his car Bibendum would be present on the various gauges and meters on the dashboard and on the guides and maps in the glove compartment; pulling into a garage he would find Bibendum on posters or advertising signs, on lockers, on air-pumps and so on. Why not, then, on restaurant menus, or on ashtrays, or on water carafes in bars? A company memorandum noted: "It was even envisaged that when he went to bed, the last thing he saw would be a Bibendum embroidered on his pyjamas or night-shirt".

Bibendum's presence was to be extended to bookshops, theatres, cinemas, dance-halls and to the most obscure items of every-day life. Among the categories that

were carefully looked into were household goods, motor accessories and garage equipment. In the end, few of these items went into production. Among those that did were the air-pump, a Saint-Claude pipe of which 144,000 were made and which were immediately snapped up, and a chocolate Bibendum made by Tobler "to the highest quality available". The chocolate mascot was an immediate favourite with children. But curiously, these unexpected commercial successes put an end to the proposed bibendumisation of the motorist's world. Producers of other brands of the items in question complained of unfair competition. Michelin would be taking away their customers, they said, and threatened to boycott Michelin tyres in reprisal. Moreover, the company's commercial structure was not organised to meet the growing demand. The brand's agents and travelling salesmen lost huge amounts of time dealing with the new orders, to the detriment of tyre sales. A decision had to be taken quickly. In 1930 Edouard Michelin and his business managers in Clermont-Ferrand ordered that all accessory production activities were to be terminated forthwith, apart from maps and guides.

Motor Show stands. Young girls in Auvergne regional dress. They carried out on-the-spot wheel repairs to demonstrate that anyone could manage such operations.
Page 65, top: *Edouard and André Michelin in the form of Michelin Men, by Georges Villa (1921).*
Bottom: *Publicity photograph, 1927.*
Page 66: *Bibendum turns up in the most ingenious forms, such as this fountain gushing water into the swimming pool of the Clermont-Ferrand Sports Association, founded by Michelin in October 1911.*

In April 1931 André Citroën organised a "Grand Tour of Asia" for several cars of standard design which had been modified for the occasion and fitted with specially made Michelin tyres. The cars were to cross the Himalayas and the Gobi desert, traverse Afghanistan, despite the rebellion in progress there, then face the uprising in Sian-Kiang, not to mention war-torn China... The vehicles headed east, with the enthusiastic blessing of André Michelin, now aged 78. But the motoring pioneer was never to see their return: he died on the morning of April 4.

The press was unanimous in its praise of him. "With his brother Edouard, André Michelin played a major role in the development of mechanical locomotion, both having been convinced and enthusiastic practitioners from the beginning, conscious of the pleasures and usefulness of motoring and having glimpsed its immense future", *Le Figaro* wrote in a long eulogy. It hailed André Michelin's modern, patriotic attitude and paid tribute to his flair for publicity: "He had a genius for original forms of propaganda that were attractive, witty, bold, image-based, but always informative and persuasive".

Another daily, *La Flamme*, began its obituary: "In the mind of the average Frenchman, Michelin was above all the famous industrialist who made outstanding tyres. Bibendum stands at every crossroads in towns and countryside, a familiar figure to the children who play there and know him as the symbol of the life's work of André Michelin".

André had been in sole charge of the company's publicity since 1910 and all his life had taken the crucial decisions regarding its public relations, even when Edouard decided to lighten his work-load by appointing a publicity chief to work under him. The job description he drafted for the proposed assistant is instructive in the way it sets out André's philosophy of advertising.

"He (the new publicity chief) must not be seduced by his own ideas and must learn to judge those of others. He must visit clients regularly and determine what most impresses them, perfect his advertising copy, strive for short, striking formulae, avoid imitating, refrain from attacking -- unless certain of success -- the advertising of rival producers, and never forget that the image is more important than the text."

It took a full year before a suitable candidate could be found to head the service responsible for the "Michelin Mondays" and the "illustrated plays", the major press campaigns of the 1920s and 1930s. Though it tried hard to recover the glories of the past, the team of draughts-men, printers and multilingual writers who formed the Michelin publicity agency, broadcasting Bibendum's message to the world, never again matched the verve and the touch of madness that had defined the company's image during André's lifetime.

"Here is the champagne, I am the bubbles", André said one day when introducing his brother. A neat turn of phrase that Edouard is said to have completed with the following rejoinder: "But without the bubbles there is no champagne".

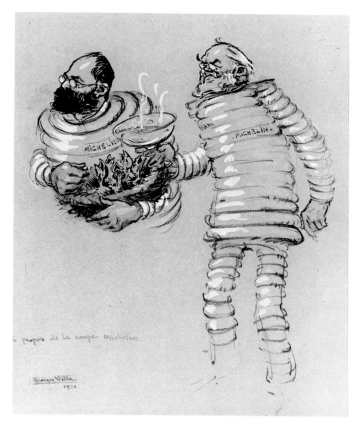

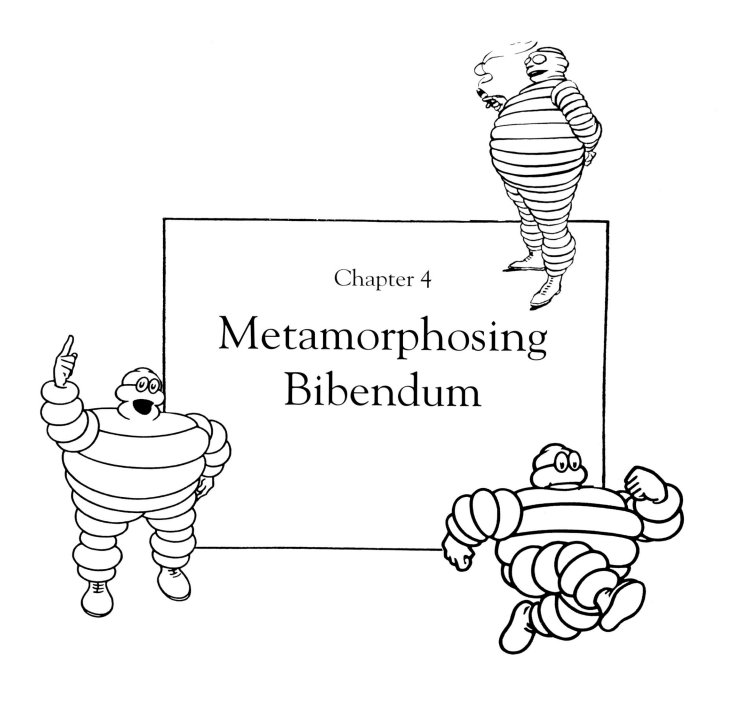

Chapter 4

Metamorphosing Bibendum

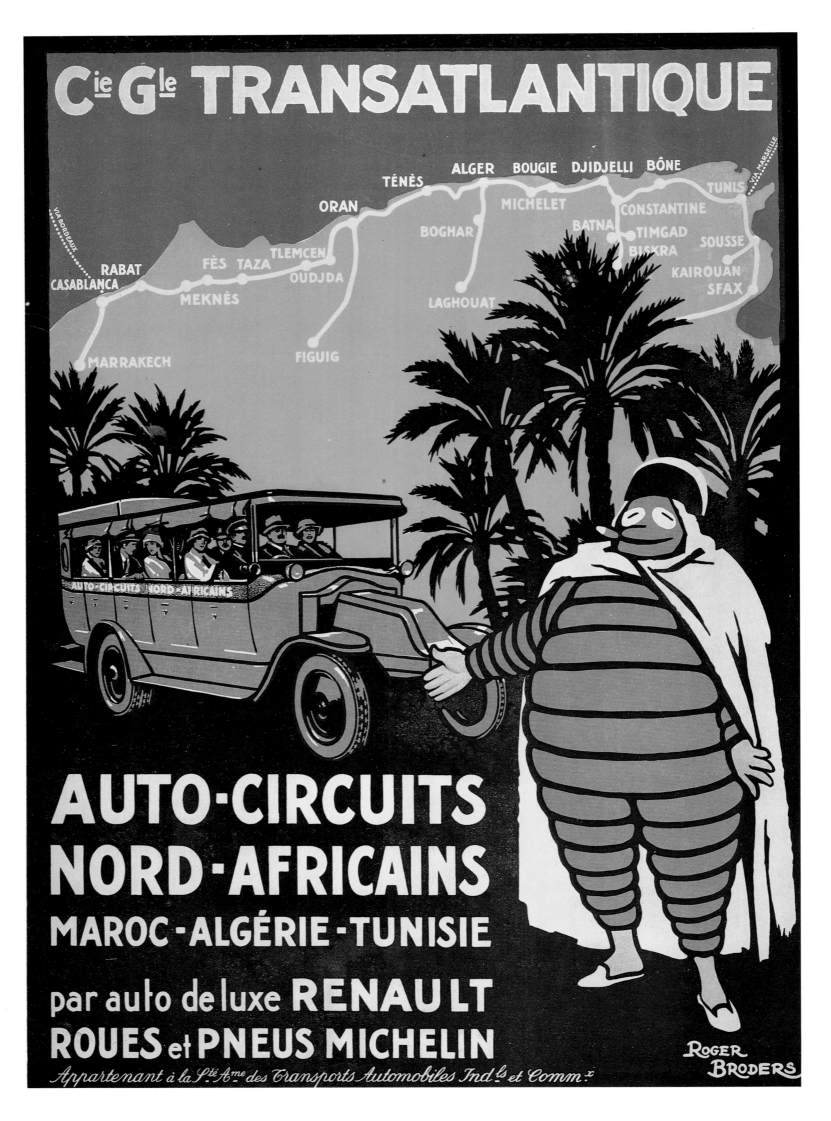

Michelin Man, known throughout France as Bibendum, was the brain-child of the graphic artist O'Galop, with André Michelin acting as midwife at his birth. In the years to come, however, the rubber man was brought to life by other artists, as if his vitality and energy demanded constant reinterpretation. Less than a year after Bibendum's first public appearance, at the Motor Show in June 1898, the inaugural issue of the *Revue Parisienne* organised a "cartoon competition to publicise the Michelin tyre".

O'Galop unsurprisingly featured among the 10 prize-winners, but in fact the top prize of 500 francs went to an artist called Stolz who presented a cartoon portraying a crocodile and a lion fighting over a tyre, with the caption: "They needn't bother -- it's a Michelin". Thus from the very beginning, the company's advertising was seen as a collective enterprise with no single artist claiming a monopoly, not even O'Galop. It is also significant that Bibendum did not feature in the winning entry. Policy was to use him regularly but by no means systematically. O'Galop, Ernest Montaut, Fraikin, Geo Ham, Fabiano and many other artists were employed to produce images from which Bibendum was absent.

Advertising mascots

The rumbustious aspects of Bibendum's character that marked his early years as the Michelin emblem were moderated over time. As the company grew larger and its advertising budget expanded, the rubber man reined in his displays of extravagant behaviour, settling down to a series of regular appearances in the daily newspapers, particularly the "Michelin Mondays". From 1901 he began to moderate his language; the objective now was to consolidate the firm's credibility and to scrupulously avoid unnecessary disputes with the competition. So while retaining his life-and-soul-of-the-party image, he displayed greater tact and less impertinence. Or at least, this was his brief for the weekly Monday outings; on the occasions when he was restored to top billing, on posters or in brochures, his restraint evaporated and he recovered his insatiable appetite for boisterous action. Bibendum's double life was the natural consequence of his role as the company mascot. Intimately associated with the brand image, and yet omnipresent, the mascot was obliged, in order to remain effective in the long term and to retain freshness, to develop a character of some complexity: fluctuating, versatile, light-hearted, unpredictable.

"I trust that no-one will be surprised if I point out how difficult it is to devise a campaign which combines the advantages of unity and originality while at the same time remaining varied", a writer for the magazine *Vendre* remarked in February 1927. A mascot is able to provide all this, he noted. "It creates unity among the various advertising techniques used; the originality of its physiognomy (take Bibendum, for example) differentiates the campaign from those of other brands; and there is variety in the situations and attitudes in which it is represented."

Specialist media during the 1910s and 1920s placed increasing emphasis on the need to create a company image, a requirement made doubly relevant by the growth

Passed on from one artist to another, Bibendum goes through endless transformations. In their immense diversity, these various, sometimes divergent treatments confer on the character a vitality he would not have achieved had the artists not been given such licence.
Page 68: *"Motoring circuits in North Africa, by Renault luxury motors, Michelin wheels and tyres", poster by Roger Broders, 1922.*
Above: *Poster for Russia, René Vincent, February 1914.*

Ved De
hvorfor jeg
ikke glír
paa vaate veíe?

MICHELIN

in advertising and the appearance of quality magazines. This was a new development in France, where since 1843 *L'Illustration* had been virtually alone at the upper end of the market for periodicals, displaying rigorous editorial standards in both form and content, printing and layout. The success of a new wave of periodicals such as *Lecture pour tous* (Reading for all, founded in 1898) and *Je sais tout* (I know everything, 1905) meant that advertisers enjoyed wider options, with new, upmarket media enabling them to bring greater sophistication and philosophical depth to such considerations as brand image. After the war, as the advertising profession became better structured and acquired a degree of technical expertise, business came under enormous pressure to rationalise and upgrade its public relations.

As the records of the national office of company names and patents show, all companies large and small were by this time equipping themselves with a logo, often in the form of a mascot. This could take the form of a mythological figure

such as a mermaid in the case of a washing machine registered in 1927, or a historical figure such as Gandhi in the case of a brand of coffee registered in Marseilles in 1931 under the name Mahatma. Animals were a popular choice. Panhard's tiger became extinct when the brand name vanished, but Peugeot's lion still prowls the jungle. The laughing cow (for the processed cheese *La vache qui rit*) and the crocodile that has become the trade-mark of Lacoste leisure-wear go back to 1921 and 1927 respectively. The vegetable world was another rich source of logos amid the plethora of names and images launched upon an unsuspecting public, as were mascots made up graphically from elements of the company's production, like Bibendum himself.

An article in the magazine *La Publicité* in 1910 devoted to the symbolism of posters openly recommended the use

Man-size or childlike, single or multiple, reassuring or threatening, Bibendum's ever-familiar silhouette is capable of myriad interpretations... From left to right: As the lone hero. "Do you know why I don't slip in mud?" this 1914 Danish poster asks. As a helpful sprite, in a 1913 brochure.
Page 71: As a fighter, O'Galop poster for the "Sole" tyre, 1905.

MICHELIN

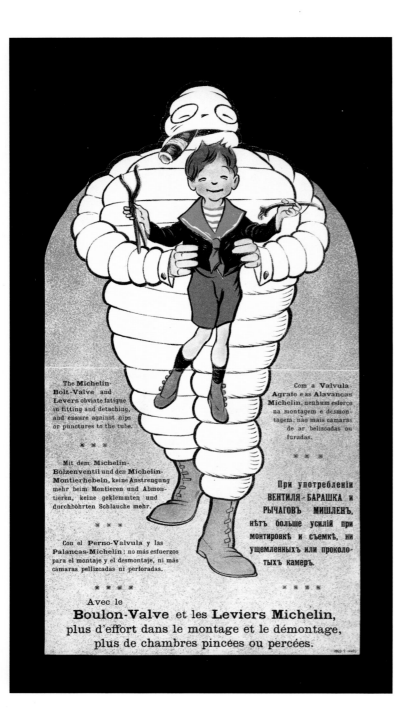

The Michelin-Bolt-Valve and Levers obviate fatigue in fitting and detaching, and ensure against nips or punctures to the tube.

* * *

Mit dem Michelin-Bolzenventil und den Michelin-Montierhebeln, keine Anstrengung mehr beim Montieren und Abmontieren, keine geklemmten und durchbohrten Schläuche mehr.

* * *

Con el Perno-Valvula y las Palancas-Michelin: no más esfuerzos para el montaje y el desmontaje, ni más camaras pellizcadas ni perforadas.

* * *

Com a Valvula Agrafe e as Alavancas Michelin, nenhum esforço na montagem e desmontagem, nao mais camaras de ar beliscadas ou furadas.

* * *

При употребленіи ВЕНТИЛЯ - БАРАШКА и РЫЧАГОВЪ МИШЛЕНЪ, нѣтъ больше усилій при монтировкѣ и съемкѣ, ни ущемленныхъ или проколотыхъ камеръ.

Avec le **Boulon-Valve** et les **Leviers Michelin**, plus d'effort dans le montage et le démontage, plus de chambres pincées ou percées.

Page 72: *Multilingual brochure,1913, illustrated by Poulbot who later the same year designed a poster for the company.*
Above: *Illustrations by Georges Bourdin, from a children's book published by Michelin in 1928.*

of anthropomorphic imagery, while warning of the dangers involved. The author, Octave-Jacques Gérin, one of the first noted theoreticians of advertising, deplored the use of pictures displaying deep cleavage, or out-and-out nudity, and gave this advice:

"Firstly the subject must be of human aspect, i.e. as far as possible it should have the appearance of a man or woman. Secondly it should contain the proposed item within itself, forming part of the human body. Finally the overall impression should be one of movement, not of immobility. (...) However, it is extremely difficult to adapt each and every product to be offered for sale to the form of the human body. (...) The bottle devised for the mint liqueur Ricqlès, with its head, arms and legs, walking like a human being (...) simply does not present the same interest. It is no more than a straightforward poster image, slightly humourous but of no symbolic value. I have to admit for my part that the difficulties involved in creating a perfect symbol are so great that I wouldn't even try. However, there are some instances of the perfect symbol.

format giving the impression that he is inert, even paralysed, creating doubts in our mind about his physical and mental health. Despite its being diametrically opposed to what we think of as the actual behaviour of small children, the image did not prevent the product from selling well. Another publicity emblem, Coca Cola's "All-American Girl", was an altogether more attractive proposition, a staple figure in the brand's advertising universe from the 1920s onwards. Even she, however, failed to gain autonomy, despite the wide range of situations in which she found herself -- with the family, with friends, out with a boyfriend, travelling by train or riding a bicycle -- and she remained in thrall to the rigid constraints that Archie Lee had set for her. Lee,

Michelin's Bibendum is a text-book example. It is the best adaptation I know, available for use in a wide variety of combinations. (...) It is not a frozen image but a lively, animated composition."

In this respect he is infinitely more autonomous than a great many publicity mascots who are his contemporaries, or near-contemporaries. For example, admittedly in a very different register, the baby adopted by Cadum soap in 1912, with his artificial smile, looks strange, as if carved out of stone. Worse than that, the repetition of his image gradually creates a malaise, his pose and the unchanging

the brand's panjandrum from the 1920s to the 1950s, set his illustrators no fewer than 35 recommendations governing the way in which the Coca Cola girl was to be presented. She was to "be aged under 20, healthy and unsophisticated, liberated and accessible" but to "avoid all excess and to act her age with eternal optimism". The result was a series of perfectly executed images, extremely homogenous, but fundamentally sterile and rather repetitive. In short, everything done strictly by the book.

One way or another, the public of the period found itself snowed under by a wave of characters made out of

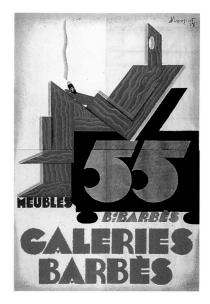

manufactured articles. Typical of these were Father Savon (soap, 1921) or Father Lustucru (spaghetti, 1920), presented as "the housewife's choice" with a huge egg-shaped torso. Others, from the world of stationery, were Carbel (1925), a man in the form of a typewriter, and the man made of pen-holders, designed in 1924 by Mich, who went on later to work for Citroën and Michelin. To these could be added a batallion of mascots made up of screws, bolts, pistons, bumpers or even sausages, or innumerable characters composed of flasks, pots, tins or bottles of medication, paint, oil, glue or polish. In 1927 O'Galop, hired to design the mascot for Siréla, a producer of floor-polish, opted for the same expedient and was roundly criticised by the magazine *La Publicité*: "We find this personification rather uninspired", the magazine wrote. "It was indeed ingenious to give the can of floor-polish the form of a man polishing a floor (...) but haven't we seen that radiant, round face, rather like a sun or a moon, somewhere before...?" How indeed was an artist to be original, given the massed ranks of anthropomorphised products placed before the public? The next wave comprised a regiment of bottles of Javel disinfectant, wine or mineral water which, like Badoit in 1927, were presented in human form. The list is endless, continuing into the 1950s and 1960s with, among the later examples, the logo of the Assimil language-teaching system, René Bravo's posters for Spontex, or the Esso character with his head in the form of an oil-drop. Even the best-known poster designers seem to have succumbed to the fashion, notably Savignac, the creator of several designs for Dunlopillo or

Dunlop, Michelin's direct competitor. At the turn of the century Dunlop tried to launch its own mascot, the Dunlopette, but in a rather half-hearted fashion, and the attempt was soon abandoned.

Forever young

What remains now of all these mascots? Sadly, very little. Few if any of the members of this happy band of mascots have survived into the present era, either because the brands they represented have disappeared, or because the brands in question failed to use them properly, or because the brands have changed them with time. Several qualities are necessary for a mascot to be able to survive the test of time: relevance, in the first instance, but also constancy and the ability to adapt to changing conditions. "It should not be solely up to the graphic artist to determine how the original design will be made up, with all subsequent artists having to conform", the magazine *Vendre* sagely observed. "The artist will want to impose his own personal mark, and perhaps at a later date the advertiser will no longer want to use him. Bibendum, whose permanent characteristics are independent of the individual artist (...) or of elements of fashion, can be drawn by any artist, and he will always be recognisable."

Bibendum's basic structure and elementary design exempt him from association with the late 19th century since, apart from his lorgnette and maybe his cigar, he has no accessories that fix him in time. Yet from his inception through to the First World War, he evolved considerably. In the series of five generic "Nunc est bibendum" posters published between 1901 and 1913, the rubber man's flat, monolithic head grew gradually rounder. During the 1910s Carlo Biscaretti, in Italy, made him slimmer, particularly

Page 74, centre: Two famous advertising characters, the Coca Cola girl of the 1920s, and the Cadum soap baby, born in 1912.
Between 1910 and 1930, numerous brand names sought to have their products associated with a publicity mascot.
Pages 74-75, above: *Miller water-bottles, 1916; Galeries Barbès furniture, C. Loupot; Dibs cigarettes, N. Fontannet, 1935; Rigal motor oil, J. d'Ylen, 1920; Barilla noodles, 1935.*

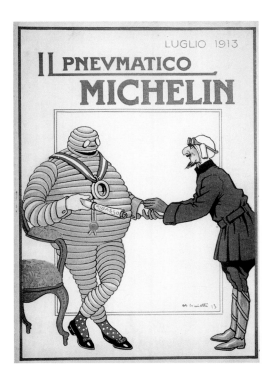

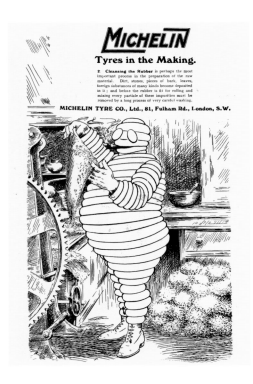

his arms and legs, often presenting him as something of a devil-may-care dandy. At the same period, the artists in Michelin's London studio were beefing him up and making him more virile. René Vincent in 1914 gave him a proper mouth and chin while two years later Fabien Fabiano drew him with fine red lips. In 1919 Albert Philibert gave his slit eyes a more human aspect, while in the United States the rubber man's expression remained minimalist, conveyed by a rough circle. These modifications, sometimes contradictory, were never taken up by the succeeding artist. There was no norm, no graphic blueprint that would fix the representation, none of the tiny variations contributed by individual artists having been specifically ordered by the advertiser. The Bibendum figure belongs to no particular artist and each is granted a degree of latitude in how he seeks to interpret him. In this way Bibendum is able to develop a repertoire of changing shapes. In 1913, for example, we find him in A. Renault's poster as a fearsome giant, with a young woman sitting in the palm of his hand, while Poulbot portrays him as a harmless fluffy doll in a small child's hand. A few years later, as drawn by Grand-Aigle in 1921, we again find him blown up to titanic proportions, this time with winged feet.

The only element that enables us to date Bibendum is his body, i.e. the tyres of which he is composed, since their width varies according to the stage of development they have reached. Over the years motor tyres became progressively wider, and in 1923, with the introduction of the "Comfort", the first low-pressure tyre to meet the road-holding and durability criteria that the public were demanding, the rubber man began to display fewer bands around his middle. Between the early designs of O'Galop and Hautot's designs in the 1920s, Bibendum's bands dwindled in number as they grew bulkier, stronger and longer-lasting, improving in quality in line with that well-known law: less is more. Thus Bibendum's body was reduced from 11 tyres to four, while his arms lost half their rings. As a result of this cosmetic surgery Bibendum's physique

became more symetrical, rigorously balanced, with both torso and limbs composed of four elements. This was to be more or less his final form.

Recast in this way, the rubber man lost the massive stature with which he began his career, becoming instead merely chubby and less threatening. Standing on shorter legs, he acquired a more boyish appearance, an aspect that became more pronounced in the years 1960-1980, when his eyes became rounder and his lorgnette was replaced by a pair of spectacles, also round. In a noted essay on evolution, American biologist and popular science writer Stephen Jay Gould unexpectedly used Bibendum as an example of what he called "neotenia", a process in which a species gradually begins to retain its youthful characteristics longer and later in the life-cycle. A Harvard professor, Gould argued that Mickey Mouse, for example, would undergo the same process as Bibendum -- his senior by 30 years -- and "withdraw into his own youth", assuming, in graphic terms, the physical characteristics of small babies. "Compared with adults", he wrote, "children have a larger head and eyes, smaller jaws, a more protuberant skull and smaller and plumper legs and feet". He concluded: "I have to say, I am afraid, that the head of the adult is more simian in every way".

Despite regressing into childhood, Bibendum nevertheless goes on smoking cigars at every opportunity. At the table, obviously, but also while playing sports of every variety, from rugby to Basque pelota, not to mention mountain-climbing. Oblivious to danger, he carries his havana even while riding a motorbike. Worse than that, he is unable to stub out his cigar even when at close quarters with a pretty girl, which must surely be the height of boorishness. However, the cigar formed an integral part of the Michelin Man's image, as can be seen by consulting the patent taken out on Bibendum back in January 1908 (an oddly late stage in his development to be securing the rights on his use). Indeed there was a kind of charm in the way in which this accessory continued to appear in even the most incongruous situations. It was not until 1929 that Michelin took steps to curb Bibendum's smoking habit, at least in the *Michelin Guide*, in line with the company's policy aimed at limiting the ravages of tuberculosis, at that

time responsible for the death of several of its employees. But like many inveterate smokers, he had periodic relapses, at least until the mid-1930s.

Bibendum's appearances, however free, extravagant and unpredictable they may have seemed, had in every case been discussed at length and prepared in detail. This emerges clearly from an exchange of letters between O'Galop and André Michelin. In January 1919 the two men met by chance on the Boulevard Pereire.

"Don't you need any more drawings?" O'Galop asked in concern. "You haven't asked me for anything for ages."

"We suspended all advertising during the war", Michelin replied. "For the moment we have no plans to resume. But... there's a poster I've been dreaming about for a long time. It shows Bibendum in a tyre."

This was how, within a few weeks of the armistice, the artist and the advertiser came

together again. O'Galop got to work immediately, and on March 12 presented André with several sketches.

Michelin was not altogether satisfied with these early drafts and the exchange of letters that followed provides a clear insight into the creative process involved in designing a poster: a sketch in chalk and charcoal, the addition

Page 76, top left to right: *Different styles of treatment mean that Bibendum has distinct qualities in each country. Elegance in Italy (cover of Michelin magazine, 1913); reassurance in the United States (newspaper advertisement, 1920); massive stature in Britain (newspaper advertisement, 1913).*
Bottom: *Two circles for glasses, a line for the mouth; a very naïve treatment of Bibendum by E.L. Cousyn who worked on the brand for several years, 1919.*
Right, from top down: *An English poster by M.L. Roowy, 1912. Albert Philibert poster, 1919.*

MICHELIN

of colour, the preparation of the actual format, all the various stages that customarily go into creating an image. In addition, the image was to be photographed, rather less usual in those days, and all the more unconventional in this case in that the photograph of a child posing in a tyre was taken not by a professional but by André's brother-in-law, who used his own child as a model.

The project, though it was finally abandoned, was typical as regards the working conditions of the time, with the advertiser organising everything and following the whole process in person from beginning to end, calling on the services of his family if necessary.

Essentially Bibendum was born of a vision by Edouard and an intuition by his brother André, made flesh by the graphic artist O'Galop; but he could be said also to owe something to Giuseppe Arcimboldo, the Italian artist who, born in Milan in 1527, is world-famous for his paintings of heads made up of fruit and vegetables, representing the four seasons. Less well-known are his paintings based on images of manufactured objects, such as "The Cook", "The Librarian" or "The Cellar-man". Admittedly the work of the painter is on a different plane from the conception of Bibendum, which was more a matter of accumulation and super-imposition than of subtle and inventive ordering of disparate objects. With the Michelin mascot, the spectator is not required to break down and reconstruct the image into anything other than what it already is. And the limited formal potential of the rubber man would have appeared rather sterile to the great painter of the imperial court.

But there is perhaps a degree of convergence between Arcimboldo's characters and Bibendum, if only with regard to the strangeness and humour that they convey. Is it not striking that Arcimboldo began his career as a designer of coats of arms, in other words as a publicity designer of his age, a hired hand working for lords and corporations? The objective of heraldic art, to strike the imagination by means of signs and symbols, is basically no different from that of the logos and mascots designed for industrial brand names.

A solitary hero

Was Bibendum a pioneer? He most certainly was as regards the design and use of mascots, in the unanimous opinion of the media of the time. Whether due to his composition, or to the fact that he was the first of a new trend, or simply because he was visible everywhere, the fact remains that he became the benchmark against which all later mascots were measured. Although all three elements undoubtedly go together, the key to the success of a mascot like Bibendum is sheer repetition. The 20,000 and more drawings of the rubber man produced between 1898 and 1930 formed a kind of propaganda barrage, as André Michelin himself was the first to admit. "The way we expose our character to our clients, present, future or lapsed (...) is, in a whole variety of unexpected ways, a kind of harassment, you could say."

Bibendum was to be found perched atop both designs of compressed-air pumps sold from 1928 onwards: the "Force" that was used in garages and the "Lumière" (light) for domestic use. With the air-tube emerging from his mouth, Bibendum breathed life back into flabby tyres, and this ingenious, humorously inventive use of the mascot helped to increase sales. "I went to visit a concessionaire called Engelbert who had been a Michelin agent some time before but had since turned against us", one travelling salesman recounted. "He'd never agreed to meet me in person previously. So one day I had the Force and the Lumière set up in his forecourt. And when Engelbert came by he stopped dead in his tracks. He saw the Bib and fell about laughing. It lowered all his defences. He asked about how the air pumps worked, wanted to know our tyre prices and said he'd think about a contract. In fact we got an order from him, his first for years, the very next day."

Was Bibendum a secret salesman? André Michelin was in no doubt that he was. As early as 1906 he commented: "As for his productive value, I reckon he is one of the key reasons why our turnover is now well over 40 million francs. It's thanks to him that our publicity has been so effective. I can prove it. We started getting more attention and attracting more interest the day we stopped using the old clichés and replaced them with Bibendum, who was infinitely more persuasive".

Two years separate these two representations of Bibendum. Over time, the giant takes on a more reassuring, almost childlike, appearance. Above: Poster by Grand-Aigle, 1921.
Page 79: From 1923 onwards, Bibendum appears much less disturbing than in his early years. He starts to lose many of the tyres that form him, in line with the new tyres appearing on the market which have a wider tread. Poster, 1927.

MICHELIN

powerful fore-arms in a way that shatters the Bibendum myth, suggesting that the god of tyres is no more than an artifice, the fairground attire of a plain man... These unpublished representations were probably no more than a private joke by the artist, a form of release in which, protected by anonymity, he indulged in the forbidden pleasures of parricide -- or at least, more prosaically, raised a laugh with his colleagues in the publicity department.

Though his achievements were many, Bibendum was as capable of aberrations as any common mortal. These were essentially due to his personality and the way he was "produced". Passing through the hands of one artist after another, he inevitably took on multiple forms, some of unequal quality, leading if not to blunders at least to all kinds of odd behaviour. One sketch for example shows him with dog's muck on his head! In the company files where it is kept hidden away -- an exhaustive record of every image ever produced by the company -- the sketch has been furiously crossed out and the words "nasty piece of work" added. Another drawing shows Bibendum as a pitiful old codger, bearded and bowed with age, struggling along on two walking sticks, virtually on his deathbed. Another shows him in shirtsleeves, baring his

Like many advertisers who have come up with a famous mascot, Michelin succumbed, momentarily, to the temptation to provide him with a family. In 1907 a drawing by O'Galop portrayed him with the following slogan: "In view of the considerable growth in sales, Bibendum has placed his son Bib in charge of the bicycle tyre branch". The experiment was not followed up, probably because it was considered too risky to divide the public's loyalty by presuming to double it. Nectar, the mascot devised by the wine firm Nicolas, was also given a family -- his wife Félicité and their child Glouglou -- but it was found he worked better as a bachelor. One artist, who has remained anonymous, succeeded in conjuring up a Mrs Bibendum, or Michelin Woman, devised as part of a campaign for a compressed air pump, showing her bottle-feeding her new-born baby. Visibly sketched in haste, the proposed spouse was not likable enough for such an illustrious husband. Finally a dog, shown running energetically at the rubber man's heels in the Grand-Aigle poster published in 1921, was the only successfully-achieved member of his fleeting household. An ebullient hero like Bibendum was really not cut out for family life.

Page 80: *This posture by Bibendum in which he is seen rolling a tyre and raising a hand in welcome is later adopted by the company as its logo. Poster by A. Philibert, 1925.*
Above: *Photographs were sometimes taken as part of the preparatory research in order to get things exactly right. Examples from the 1920s.*

continuous!

Thousands of different drawings of Bibendum were made, some of them very amusing, such as this rather unappealing Michelin Woman, or this drawing of the "drinker of obstacles" in a state of inebriation clinging to a lamp-post as if it were a life-belt.

Page 84: Undated sketches presenting the Michelin mascot in a variety of national dress guises.

Chapter 5

The World according
to Bibendum

Michelin's rapid growth from 1900 onwards was sustained by expansion into foreign markets. Already by the turn of the century the company was present in much of Europe, with concessionaires in Belgium, Austria, the Netherlands, Switzerland, Germany and Spain. The next step was to set up production units in these markets, and this got under way in 1906 in Turin, where Michelin set up its first factory outside France. Bibendum's ties with the Italian peninsula were to become particularly close.

Headed by Adolphe Daubrée, a descendant of one of the founders of the Barbier et Daubrée company, Michelin's Italian subsidiary displayed undoubted originality in its advertising. In 1907, the Agenzia Italiana Pneumatici Michelin launched a monthly magazine which it mailed to its customers. Of modest format but extremely well illustrated, *Il Pneumatico Michelin* astutely combined the main characteristics of the company's advertising policy, providing a blend of information with entertainment in line with the magazine's subtitle, "Tips and marvels from Bibendum". This lively, elegant periodical, borrowing items from the "Michelin Mondays" and the "illustrated plays", also published a charming short story each month as its leading article. This story, signed by Bibendum and written in the first person, gave the character the dimension of a fictional hero and a consistency that neither posters nor press advertisements could convey.

Bibendum at the Ball of Nations

Thus it was that the magazine's readers were invited to share in Bibendum's triumph at the social event of the year, the "Ball of Nations". Although he wore a masque, Bibendum was recognised immediately and surrounded by lovely young women garbed in the traditional dresses of a variety of nations. "A chorus of 20, 30 or 50 voices, each as melodious as the next, rose to greet me: Come, Bibendum! Irresistible, adorable! What a sweet man! We want Bibendum! Long live Bibendum!... What could I do but drop my pointless subterfuge and face up to the situation as bravely as I could, as is my wont in such circumstances, however unexpected."

The reluctant Casanova, surrounded by suitors, passed from one to the other, sharing his favours among them. Turning to the delightful creature representing

France, with sprightly wit and charm he said: "Are you not my betrothed? Why should you fear that I might neglect you? You know your Bibendum too well to think such hurtful thoughts". With Italy, he waxed lyrical: "Oh you sublime Madonna, Rome's destiny, accept my homage, you whose eyes shine with the splendours of the Renaissance. We have loved each other since the day we met. You promised to be true to me, and I, like a knight of old, pledge you my trophies". To the flaxen-haired Germany, who comes to whisper sweet words in his ear, he is soothing: "I understand your impatience. Your Bibendum is not unworthy of your valorous traditions. He drinks and he fights as in the good old days, overcomes obstacles, savours victories, and empties the goblets". Then it is England's turn, then Africa comes, then America. And to each of them he declares his ardour and plights his troth. And then the dancers form a large circle around him and the moral of the story, with its pacifist echoes, is made evident: "But did you

Page 86: *Front page of* Bibendum, *the company's Italian monthly magazine, 1931. In 1931 Michelin launched the first railcar on tyres, later to become famous as the "Micheline". This light, 24-seater vehicle could travel faster than a train.*
Above: *The Michelin agency in Italy.*

IL PNEUMATICO
MICHELIN
GENNAIO - FEBBRAIO 1912

not know that Italy was escorted here by Turkey, that England formed a couple with Germany, that Russia was on the arm of Japan?".

In this story, the Italian Bibendum is a self-appointed diplomat, reconciling adversaries by his mere presence, a redoubtable though resolutely modest seducer, a lord contemplating the world at his feet. Like a Don Juan he relishes, in the epilogue, the grim faces of his rivals, "ashen-faced suitors with fixed smiles, living symbols of a shattered illusion".

This typically Mediterranean Bibendum displayed, in his transalpine adventures, a fanciful quality even more irreverent, if possible, than that of his French counterpart. He began to subvert the heroes of Italian history, for example removing the statue of Emmanuel Philibert and taking his place on his plinth in

More than in any other country, advertising by the Agenzia Italiana Pneumatici Michelin discovered ingenious ways of exploiting the Michelin mascot.
From left to right: Front page of Il Pneumatico Michelin, 1912. Italian poster, 1931.
Below: An exemple of Bibendum's relaxed Mediterranean style. He is seen here sharing a drink and a chat with Napoleon.
Page 89: Bibendum, globe-trotting through Egypt, on the cover of the magazine Bibendum, Italy, 1922.

Turin. Charles the Fifth of Spain's hardy warrior, nicknamed "ironhead", did not of course take kindly to being dismounted.

"Bibendum, how dare you!", he expostulated.

"You're a figure from the age of iron", Bibendum replied calmly. "We now live in the age of rubber. The world has moved on. (...) In your time you overcame obstacles with the sword. Now we simply take them in our stride, by peaceful means. And I'm the one who won this battle. You forged the greatness of Piedmont; for my part I have spread the name of Michelin all over the world."

More than in France, Bibendum appears here to be set on a worldwide campaign, probably because he feels he is already on foreign soil. This is the clear message sent by an illustration portraying a tyre wrapped up in the French, Italian, American and British flags, over the caption: "The greatest invention of the century". The statement is less peremptory than might appear, seen in the light of Edouard Michelin's dictum that "the automobile is merely an accessory of the tyre", by which he

meant to highlight what a revolution it truly was to be able to travel on air and thus to reach speeds that were unthinkable with solid tyres, finally achieving the full potential of the horseless carriage. The image expresses the measure of Bibendum's power and makes explicit the collective commitment of all nations to the sovereignty of the tyre. It also explains the decision to create a temple to his cult, the baroque palace adopted as company headquarters in the heart of London, then the hub of world trade.

Michelin House

The British market, protected by the Dunlop patents, did not open properly to foreign competition until the autumn of 1904, when the patents legally expired. During the year, a small office was rented in Sussex Place to prepare the creation of the Michelin Tyre Company Limited. The market, buoyed up by Britain's economic power inherited from the Victorian era, was extremely promising, all the more so given that at the time it was dominated by French and German manufacturers. The embryonic British automobile industry had offered plenty of scope for importers of foreign-made vehicles and accessories in order to meet the burgeoning demand. Already by 1907 British car ownership was the biggest in Europe, with 53,000 vehicles registered, well ahead of France, with 31,000 vehicles, and Germany with 16,000.

Michelin Tyre Co. Ltd. was incorporated on May 11, 1905. The twin challenge of a potentially huge market and a powerful local competitor, namely Dunlop, provided a major stimulus, and chairman André Michelin decided to

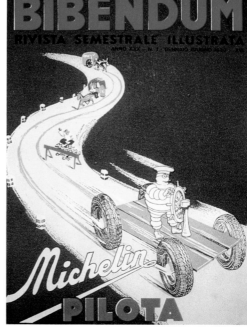

build a headquarters that gave the full measure of the company's ambitions: Michelin House. This edifice, a three-dimensional declaration of intent, a call to battle written in concrete, was inaugurated in London's Chelsea district in January 1911. Ostensibly the building was just a block of offices; in fact it was a monument to the glory of Bibendum, the rubber man who from the outset had taken a mischievous pleasure in mocking the opposition. The facade was an astonishing Art Nouveau interpretation of the company's traditional advertising themes. Located at the junction of Fulham Road, Sloane Avenue and Lucan Place, it offered passers-by the spectacle of gigantic stained-glass windows each displaying one of the firm's publicity posters. In the centre over the front entrance, the largest of the windows presented Bibendum as portrayed in the "Nunc est bibendum" series, standing at the table with his glass raised, full of its gargantuan libation of nails and pieces of glass. Overlooking Lucan Place, he appeared on a bicycle, carefree and full of beans, chomping on his cigar, with a happy-go-lucky air dia-

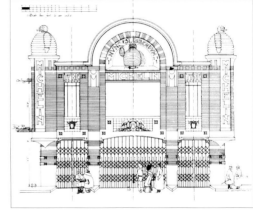

metrically opposed to the aggressive aspect he presented to Sloane Avenue. Here he appeared in O'Galop's famous low-angle image of a French kick-boxer, his best foot forward in a style banned under British boxing laws. To devote a whole panel of glass-work to a foreign conception of sporting manners was indeed to carry the battle to the enemy.

In keeping with the company's advertising policy, Michelin House was unusually bold in a London context where the use of colour in architecture was still relatively rare. The press enthused over the beauty of the ceramic facade, the richness of the colours and the abundance of

the ornamentation in which the tyre motif was predominant. The obsessive repetition of the company's monogram and the numerous other typographic extravagancies created an impression of saturation, a tangled hybrid of indefinite status and dual personality. Was this the distinguished head office of an honourable and prosperous manufacturing company, as the richness of the materials might lead the observer to believe? Or was it a fairground stand on which an unbridled imagination had been let loose in order to achieve the maximum impact?

The early sketches and architectural plans clearly indicate that the extravagant design was intentional and had been worked out at length. Though the execution patently had to tone down some aspects of the design in order to meet local authority requirements, the project nonetheless succeeded in achieving its initial objective. According to local residents at the time, it was at night that Michelin House displayed all its excesses and its true nature. Perched on two turrets, the glass cupolas cast their intense yellow light out into the darkness, while the central stained-glass window, back-lit by a mercury lamp, glowed a grey-blue marble tint, bathing Bibendum in an aura that was both ghostly and titanic.

The structure of Michelin House, so spectacularly built around company motifs, undoubtedly made it a kind of advertisement in glass and concrete, a genre that -- apart from the pavilions at the universal exhibitions of the time -- had no precedent. Only in the 1920s did it acquire a degree of recognition, drawing the attention of avant-garde artists such as Rodchenko, Mayakovsky or Fortunato Depero for whom commercial

Page 90: *Designed as posters, the front pages of* Il Pneumatico Michelin, *renamed* Bibendum *after the First World War, received particularly close attention; a trend initiated by artist Carlo Biscaretti (1899-1959).*
Centre: *The company's British headquarters, Michelin House, a paean in three dimensions to Bibendum, was inaugurated in 1911. In his early drafts, the architect had envisaged topping the building's turrets with huge sculptures of the Michelin mascot.*

BIBENDUM

architecture need not represent a compromise or loss of integrity. In the following decades the conception caught on and finally took off, particularly in the design of petrol stations, though in an infinitely more modest register. The new forms were initially caricatures of traditional designs, such as the country pavilion or mountain chalet, then gradually acquired greater originality, until the petrol stations found their own formal vocabulary, metaphors for speed and service. The play of the volumes of painted concrete, punctuated with outsize luminous logos, composed a veritable three-dimensional poster, a semaphore message to the motorist.

The exuberance of the Michelin House architecture formed not so much a poster as a hymn to the tyre, an exhaustive panegyric of the company's heroic age. Around the side of the building and the entrance hall, 34 ceramic panels relate the major events and sporting victories with which Michelin tyres have been associated, from Charles Terront's Paris-Brest-Paris exploit to the Michelin brothers' expedition from Paris to Bordeaux and back, from the Gordon Bennett Cup to the Saint Petersburg-Moscow rally. With immense finesse, the designs convey the constant pursuit of speed and the tension involved, the fierce concentration of the drivers, with their creased faces as they pass through clouds of dirt, the inexpressible thrill experienced by the pioneers of motor-racing in the early years of the century.

Conquering the British market

The motor car in those days was an item of luxury and pleasure, not designed for merely utilitarian purposes. It was a symbol of opulence for those carefree and frivolous enough to enjoy the abundance and prosperity of the closing years of the Edwardian era. Bibendum's early attentions were therefore directed at the gentleman driver, whom he addressed in a somewhat didactic man-

ner. Having presented his products and discussed them with his prospective client, Bibendum would gradually harden his tone, little by little discarding the airs and graces of the well-bred teacher. The price war with Dunlop was drawing out Bibendum's irreverent instincts. A full-page newspaper advertisement in 1913, with the slogan "An irresistible rise in popularity", symbolised the rubber man's determination to get ahead, to acquire greater assurance and greater substance. Sir Bibendum, as he was now called, then featured in a series of advertise-

ments in *The Autocar* magazine, which presented him gracing the company of the good and the great, for example addressing the House of Lords, where his speech received a burst of applause.

Unlike in France, the outbreak of the First World War failed to dent the upsurge in advertising in Britain. On the contrary: it acted as a stimulus, inspiring impassioned statements of patriotic fervour. The last months of 1914 saw the launch of a massive press campaign vaunting the "Entente Cordiale", a testimony to the strength of the bond between the two countries.

"The English and the French are brothers in arms. Our allied colours are nailed to the mast. The British navy

Details of Michelin House. A panel of ceramic tiles. A mosaic in the entrance hall.
Page 93, from left to right: *British newspaper advertisement issued after the close of the 1912 Motor Show. Brochure cover, 1910.*

protects the seas, and the supply of Michelin tyres will be maintained. Vive l'Angleterre! France for ever! Three cheers: hurrah! hurrah! hurrah!"

An exultant Bibendum entwines the French and British flags in a sign of victory. Looking far into the future, he envisages a tunnel under the Channel, made up of car tyres. But however sincere the tribute may have been, the display of unity before the common enemy did not necessarily mean a truce on the tyre sales front. An advertisement published in 1915 showed an ambulance

After the Show
MICHELIN

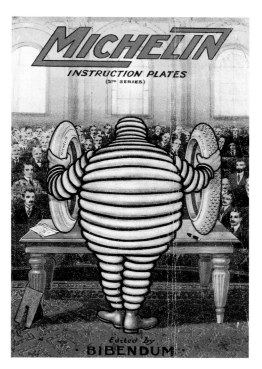

MICHELIN
INSTRUCTION PLATES
(2ᵐᵉ SERIES)

Edited by
· BIBENDUM ·

with punctured tyres being repaired by a team of Michelin mechanics. The hard-hitting caption gave the reader to understand that the problem with the defective tyres (which bear a strong pictural resemblance to Dunlop tyres!) arose from the manufacturer's parsimony with rubber.

Bibendum's life across the Channel was thus different in many ways from that in his homeland. The constant awareness of the threat posed by his indigenous rival made him more irascible, required him to be ever on the alert. The particular nature of the British market -- large, competitive, strategic and geographically close -- led the company to undertake an experiment that was unusual for its time, at least in Europe where marketing tests and surveys were a great deal less developed than in the United States.

In order to gain some idea of the precise impact of advertising on sales, Michelin decided in 1925 to concentrate its entire advertising effort on a single region. A huge campaign was launched in the test area, the county of Durham, focusing solely on the firm's reputation, deliberately abstaining from promotional activities (such as the lowering of prices) and from special announcements such as proclaiming the development of an innovation or a new product. The idea was that employing only institutional advertising, the company would obtain a laboratory-exact assessment of the effect of publicity.

"The way we figured it," a Michelin official said, "without publicity, sales in Durham would reflect the general level of sales in Britain as a whole. They were arguably a little below the national average because it was a mining region, badly hit by the economic recession. So our advertising in the region would be the only differentiating factor. Any changes in the sales pattern which we observed would be due solely to advertising. So to measure the results, we calculated the quotient each month of sales in the Durham region divided by sales in the British isles overall."

The operation was launched on December 1, 1925 and conducted over a full year. The key to the campaign was a weekly advertisement in a range of newspapers calculated to reach 95 percent of the car-owning population, along with a variety of other initiatives such as monthly mail-shots, regular promotional activities in concessionaires' shop-windows and Michelin screen advertisements shown in cinemas. Added to this was a travelling publicity team which crisscrossed the region on a regular basis. The results at year's end spoke volumes: local sales up by 80 percent. A later report indicated that sales in the county of Durham continued to perform better than anywhere else in Britain even five years after the one-year campaign was discontinued.

The globe-trotter

By now Bibendum and the promotional teams accompanying him as he paraded before groups of happy children handing out gimmicks and brochures had cast

WHEN THE TRUTH IS TOLD

1155 DUNLOP TYRES FITTED AT OLYMPIA

ACTUAL FIGURES regarding tyres fitted to cars at Olympia:—

BRITISH DUNLOPS	1155	GERMAN TYRES	541
OTHER BRITISH TYRES	76	AMERICAN TYRES	24
FRENCH TYRES	707	ITALIAN TYRES	9

Above: Competition in Britain between Dunlop and Michelin was fierce, as indicated by this Dunlop advertisement portraying a microscopic Bibendum. Page 95: Michelin's advertising in Britain in 1914 is resolutely triumphalist. Nothing can stop Bibendum, who builds a tunnel out of tyres under the English Channel, symbolising the indissoluble ties between the two countries.

G·DUCREY
ENTREPOSITAIRE MICHELIN à BUCAREST

their net far beyond the mining towns of Northern England or the beaches of France. The rubber man had become a familiar figure around the world. *Bibendum*, Michelin's in-house journal in France during the years 1929-30, published an exhaustive survey of his appearances around the globe. Here he was now in Chile, straddling a motorcycle, here now in Seville, perched on the back of a cart below the city walls, now strolling along the Malecon, Havana's sea-front boulevard, now in Syria, on the road to Damascus, or before the Golden Temple in Amritsar in northeast India, or in the Irrawaddy valley in Burma...

Following in Bibendum's footsteps, Michelin's agents set up sales campaigns and attempted to organise local distribution networks, which, in the remote outposts that some of these places then were, sometimes spurred them to prodigious feats of improvisation. "Mr Thomas, our agent in Siam", the journal reported, "was rapidly brought up against the hard facts of rail travel in the region: timetables that bore only an occasional relation to reality, connections that would require long hours, or sometimes days, of waiting. And what else was there to do while waiting around in a station in some remote hill-town, if you were a salesman, but to get out and sell? And thus somehow the trains always seemed to arrive too soon. Faced with waiting in a waiting room for two hours for the next train, Mr Thomas preferred to get out into the streets and down to work, selling his tyre pressure gauges to local motorists and taxi-drivers."

Sometimes events conspired to create dangerous confusion, as was the case in Bombay under the British Empire where the Michelin mascot was caught up in the turmoil of a local conflict. In 1929, the regional representative recounted, there was a sudden surge of unrest, in the course of which Bibendum was the involuntary cause of a misunderstanding that almost had fatal consequences. "Twenty deaths a day, fifty wounded. For a whole week, our agents kept their shutters down. (...) The cause of the fighting, as usual, was ethnic differences, the immediate pretext was a story put about by

the Hindu community accusing Bombay's Pathans (Moslems) of kidnapping children in order to sacrifice them. (...) This story got us into some deep water. The van used by our local dealers bore a picture of a family of Bibendums painted on the side. As it drove through the bazaar on its way to make a delivery, it was set upon by a group of rioters who said it was the van used to kidnap Hindu children, as proved by the picture of the baby Bibendum on the side."

Bibendum the bogey-man, the scapegoat offered to appease the anger of the crowd: a world away from the United States, where a production unit had been established as far back as 1908. Under the influence of

American methods, Bibendum's advertising strategy across the Atlantic was based on "scientific" principles. Though the designs, with their broad swathes of colour, were successful, the advertisements were based on the tried and tested formula in which typography, text and product presentation were balanced one against the other, enhancing readability but often reducing the vitality of the central character. However, when in Rome, do as the Romans do -- this has long been Bibendum's rule of thumb in his campaign of world conquest. A rule applied in this case to undeniable effect, since for most American consumers there was little doubt as to Bibendum's nationality: he was American. A maestro in Italy, he was also a "sir" in Britain or a bullfighter in Spain, effectively a chameleon, and even if not specifically adapted to the local culture, he was invariably adopted by the local population, becoming an object of great affection. Thus a photograph taken in Algeria shows a garage-owner posing proudly next to a Bibendum whom he has crowned with a fez. After all, the bare-headed mascot surely needed protection against the harsh rays of the North African sun... What other publicity mascot would inspire such thoughtful attention?

Page 96, bottom: *"Michelin retailers can be found all over the world. On this side, 3,000 retailers"* -- *a Latin American plaque, 1913.*
Above: *The company's globe-trotters, Michelin representatives who travel all over the world and often encounter unexpected situations.*
Pages 98-99 and 100-101: *Esthetically successful, the balanced composition of these American posters of 1910 presents a different face of Bibendum. Here he adopts a more rational line, seen as more effective.*

MICHELIN
UNIVERSAL CORD

A Sturdy, Oversize Cord Tire that Establishes a New Standard for Supreme Durability and Freedom from Skidding

The Michelin Universal Cord embodies three substantial improvements in cord tire construction: *first*, a new and perhaps unequalled wear-resisting tread-compound; *second*, an improved non-skid tread that offers effective protection against skidding in every possible direction; *third*, a super-sturdy oversize body. These combined advantages result in increased efficiency and a freedom from blow-outs hitherto unknown. For your next tire get a Michelin Universal Cord.

Michelin Tire Company, Milltown, New Jersey
Other factories: Clermont-Ferrand, France; London, England; Turin, Italy
Dealers in all parts of the world

MICHELIN
UNIVERSAL CORD

Sure footed on all roads and in all kinds of weather

A sturdy, oversize cord tire that establishes a new standard for durability and freedom from skidding.

MICHELIN TIRE COMPANY - MILLTOWN, NEW JERSEY

Other factories: Clermont-Ferrand, France; London, England; Turin, Italy. — Dealers in all parts of the world.

3,000,000 are MICHELINS

How to Change to Michelin Comfort Balloons
one tire at a time

Next time you need a tire, buy a Michelin Comfort Balloon and mount it as a spare. Then when you put this spare into use, buy a second Michelin Comfort Balloon and put the two balloons on your rear wheels. Repeat the process on front wheels. If, in the meantime, it becomes necessary for you to run with a Michelin Comfort Balloon and a high pressure tire opposite one another, you can do so temporarily without harm or inconvenience.

Michelin makes Comfort Balloon tires for present rims and the new small-diameter wheels. Also high-pressure tires and the famous Michelin Ring Shaped Tube.

MICHELIN TIRE COMPANY
Milltown, New Jersey

From Spain to Cuba, from Ceylon to Tehran, Bibendum takes up position around the globe.
Page 102, from top down and from left to right: *Bibendum in Mexico (1929), Football team in France (1929),*
Bibendum conducting a band at Harrow (UK, 1925). A Michelin van in Salonica (Greece, 1952), a neon sign
in Tehran (Iran, 1951), a Morris car in a hill race in Ceylon (1952).
Above, from top down and from left to right: *Bibendum in London (UK, c. 1926), in Amsterdam (1930),*
in Pakokku (Burma, 1930), Bibendum parade in Japan (c. 1930) and in Hong Kong (1952).
Page 104: *Italian hoarding at the Monza race-track near the popular stands, 1952.*

Chapter 6

Bibendum
goes
on holiday

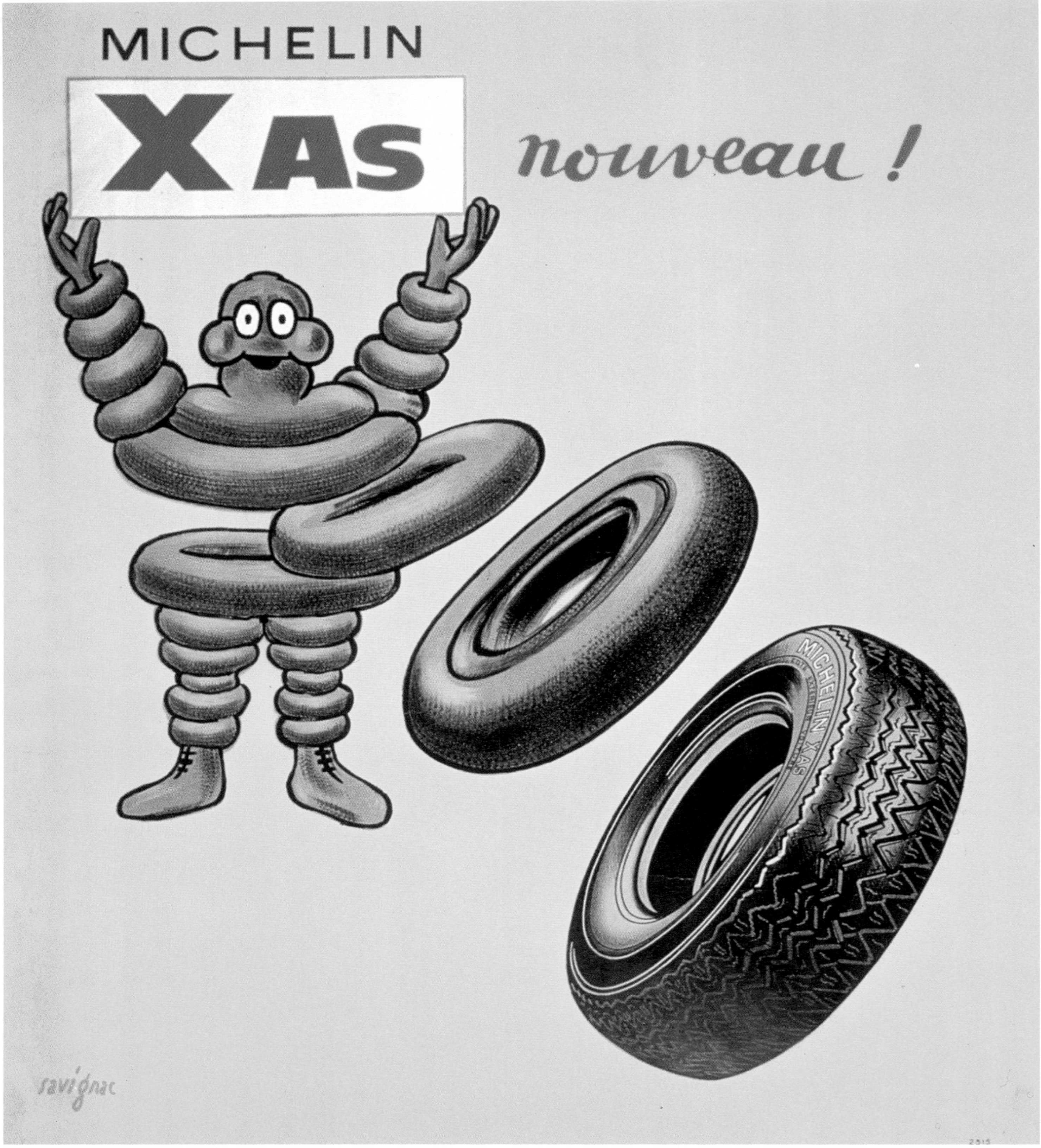
MICHELIN
X AS
nouveau !
MICHELIN X AS
savignac

When Edouard Michelin died in August 1940, at the ripe old age of 81, Robert Puiseux and Pierre Boulanger were appointed to run a company which by then had innumerable ramifications abroad. Between 1931 and 1937 it had set up factories in Germany, Argentina, Spain, Czechoslovakia and Belgium, ensuring that Bibendum had plenty of foreign travel in prospect. In France however, the German occupation meant that supplies were becoming increasingly problematic. In view of the general shortage of raw materials, the company turned its skills to recycling its products on behalf of a population that was experiencing increasing material difficulties: making sandals out of old tyres, brooms, wire brushes, gas engines and wood-fuelled stoves.

When will we be able to afford a car?

After the war, as the cities destroyed by aerial bombardment were slowly rebuilt, the acquisition of a motor car remained an impossible dream for most French families, many of them still living in temporary accommodation. When will we be able to afford a car?, was the recurrent question. For the most realistic families, the best hope appeared to be the new low-cost model designed by Citroën, the 2CV, or "*deux-chevaux*", advertised as "a real car with four real seats and four doors, carrying four people and 110 pounds of luggage at 40 miles an hour". To encourage potential purchasers, it added: "The essentials-yes! Luxury-no!". The price, however, remained a significant deterrent. At 250,000 francs, it cost around half the annual income of the average French household.

In those early post-war years, with France still in the firm grip of austerity, the consumer society appeared a remote aspiration rather than an imminent reality. Compared with the United States, which by now had taken over from Europe as the world's leading economic power, the level of household comfort in France was modest in the extreme. The first priority for most middle-class families was a refrigerator, the "cold-box" which would enable them to keep butter and other dairy foods from going off. Even so, only 17 percent of households owned

one at a time when 96 percent of households in America were so equipped. Similarly, whereas in the United States one in four households owned a car, in France the figure was one in 17. While the Americans were cruising around in their powerful, sleek, chromium-plated Cadillacs, Chryslers and Fords, the best most French people could hope for was a Renault 4CV, a four horse-power family saloon that resembled a toad in comparison.

Times were hard for Michelin too in those early post-war years. The company's stand alongside the Allies had cost it dearly. For Robert Puiseux, Edouard Michelin's son-in-law and now company chairman, the need was to rebuild the firm and in this regard he had every reason to be confident.

The X revolution

Puiseux's high hopes for the future were founded on a new tyre design, a promising innovation devised by Marius Mignol, one of his engineers who had tried to make profitable use of his enforced leisure during the war. His idea was simple: why not change the arrangement of the sheets of criss-crossed cords that form the body of a tyre, so that they no longer form different angles but are disposed radially, in other words in such a way that the radiuses form hoops perpendicular to the tread. The new structure not only doubles the working life of the tyre but also combines vertical elasticity, smoothing out the unevenness of the road's surface, with the horizontal rigidity needed for effective road-holding. This revolutionary development, the radial

Page 106: *This poster by Savignac (1965) is the only known example showing Bibendum breaking down into his component tyres.*
From top down: *Plaque on wood-fuelled stoves produced by Michelin during World War II. Danish poster, around 1960. German poster, 1972.*

tyre marketed under the name Michelin X, gave the company a technological lead of several years over all its main rivals.

However, Michelin was unable to profit fully from this invention, which has since become the norm for tyres. This is no doubt one of the reasons why Bibendum seems to have been relegated for a number of years to a secondary role. How indeed was the company to keep up with the growth in automobile production at a time of general scarcity? This was the circle that François Michelin, Edouard's grandson who became managing director in 1955, had to square. One of his top priorities was to increase the company's production capacity. To this end he opened 15 new factories within the space of 15 years, between 1955 and 1969.

For a while the company found itself in the paradoxical situation of enjoying an indisputable advance over its competitors, while having considerable difficulties in meeting market demand. It found itself forced to reverse its usually pro-active advertising strategy and to adopt a more conventional profile. Times were changing, moreover, and it was no longer good enough merely to fire off salvoes at the competition. The advertising profession was better organised, rejuvenated and newly confirmed in its advisory role to industry as a key player in the economic process. The advertiser "is no longer, as before, the man called in at the last minute, as a last resort; he is no longer seen as a kind of medicine man whose services are called upon when all else has failed. (...) He has become a witness and a participant in the whole chain of decision-making", wrote Marcel Bleustein-Blanchet, founder of the Publicis agency, in his memoirs. It was an irony of history that Bibendum found himself

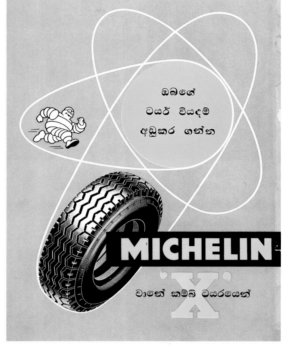

sidelined just at the moment when French advertising began to acquire a degree of credibility with the general public and intellectuals such as Roland Barthes and Jean Baudrillard began taking a serious interest in advertising as a subject of sociological and anthropological inquiry.

"After the war, the difficulties we had in meeting demand were such that our advertising had to be restrained for the simple reason that despite the potential market we had little to sell", the marketing chief at the time commented. "It took us quite a while to even out this imbalance. As late as the early 1970s, the sales people were telling us not to push our products so hard. Our customers, the retailers, would have found it absurd had we done so, since we were still practising a kind of rationing in meeting orders. For example if a retailer ordered 50 units of a given item, we would only deliver 30. These were strange times when, in spite of everything I have just said, new factories were springing up everywhere to meet a surge in sales of the order of 15 percent per year."

Through all this Bibendum remained effectively silent, or nearly so, away from the public gaze. This at least, with a few exceptions, was the general impression given by the discretion with which he merged into the background and muted his previous combativeness and irreverence. He seemed to have thrown in the towel, an unlikely fate for the mascot of a company whose sales were continuing to grow. Had he passed his sell-by date? That was the growing impression of at least some of the 20 graphic artists, designers and artistic directors employed in the Michelin studio, the in-house publicity department that handled all the company's public relations.

"None of the artists enjoyed working on Bibendum any more. No-one in the studio drew any inspiration from him, and no-one really knew how to draw him. We'd all gone off him completely. We found him old hat, old-fashioned, old everything", the studio chief of the time recalled. But suddenly, on July 21, 1969, something happened that proved them wrong. On that day, television screens around the world broadcast the historic images of Neil Armstrong

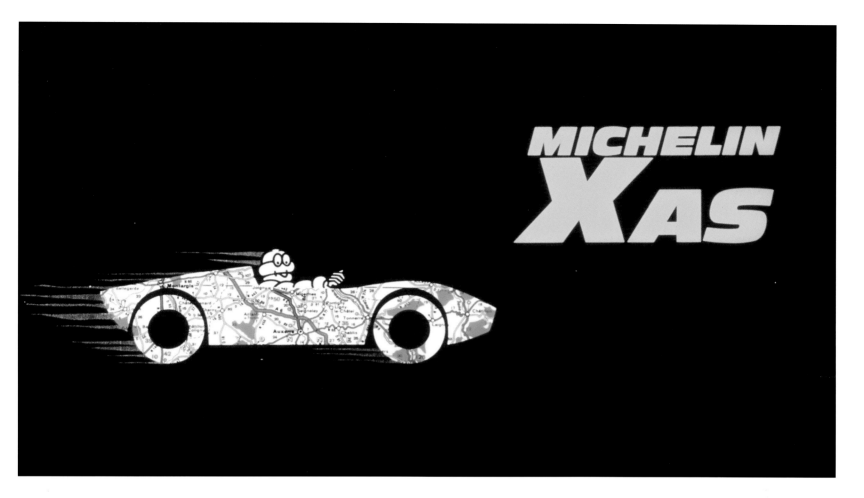

and Edwin Aldrin, the astronauts of the Apollo 11 mission, taking their first hesitant steps on the moon, shrouded in huge white space-suits which, in France at least, instantly reminded everyone of Bibendum. In the newspapers, at the office or in the local café, Bibendum was the name on people's lips whenever the heroes of the day were mentioned. Describing Aldrin's movements in the attenuated gravity of the moon's surface, the television commentator said: "His enormous space-suit makes him look like a Bibendum". Michelin's rubber man thus found himself associated with the conquest of space, the event of the century, the triumph of technology -- not bad for a has-been.

The sudden loss of interest in Bibendum was a specifically French phenomenon, since in Italy, following the massive impact which the moon venture created, he was sent to the moon in an advertising cartoon, while in the United States he embarked on a promising new career. Bibendum derived significant advantage from the road-safety campaign launched by Ralph Nader, the bold young lawyer who took on the US automobile industry for, in his view, cynically sacrificing safety considerations in the pursuit of profit. Bringing scientific rigour to bear in his analysis, Nader highlighted the flaws and inconsistencies in automobile production,

demonstrating to the public that their gleaming roadsters were in fact mobile coffins lacking the most elementary safety precautions.

Among the dangers that Nader brought to public attention was the poor road-holding qualities of American cars, and in this regard he also had harsh things to say about US tyre manufacturers, whom he accused of turning out mediocre products unadapted to the weight of the vehicles. His indictment struck a chord with the public and the media and Michelin emerged with its credit considerably enhanced, being singled out as a reliable brand whose product was long-lasting and rarely blew out. From that point on, within the space of barely 10 years, the company patiently built up its clientele in North America and carved out a growing reputation for its products. Caterpillar, the world leader in construction site vehicles, Ford, with the Mustang and later

During the 1950s and 1960s, Bibendum was largely sidelined, rarely playing more than a secondary role. This was the time when artist Jean Effel drew a slender, deflated Bibendum (page 108, bottom) who appeared distinctly anxious about his future.
Page 108, top: *Ceylon poster, 1960.*
From top down: *French poster, 1965. Moroccan poster, 1958.*

other top-of-the-range vehicles, soon fitted all their vehicles with Michelin tyres, and Sears & Roebuck, America's largest mail-order firm, included them in its catalogue.

Bibendum was naturally part of the process. Building up gradually, the company's advertising budgets of the period reached levels far and away above those of the turn of the century when Michelin made its first incursion into this huge market, setting up its first factory in the United States in Milltown before falling foul of the 1929 crash.

The Red Bible

Though France in the 1950s, as an economic power, lagged far behind the United States, whose motor industry accounted for almost 80 percent of world production, it had nonetheless achieved steady growth. The emphasis on post-war reconstruction meant that the spread of motoring was slowed, but Michelin's in-house bulletin, celebrating the brand's 50th anniversary and half a century of tourism, was still able to note that "everyone is driving". Since its first publication in 1900, Michelin's famous red guide had become a best-seller far beyond France's borders. The publication of a guide to Belgium in 1904 had inaugurated a series covering a large part of Northern Europe (Switzerland, the Netherlands, Germany, Britain) and the Mediterranean region (Italy, Spain, Portugal, Algeria, Tunisia, Egypt), catering for customers in all those countries where sales were growing.

Between 1946 and 1960, the number of new car registrations per year in Europe increased by a factor of 10. Demand for Michelin's guide, by now the standard reference, naturally rose in proportion. This extract from an article by *Time* magazine in 1961 gives an indication of the guide's renown:

"It has become France's gastronomic bible, capable of making and destroying the reputation of restaurants from Paris to the

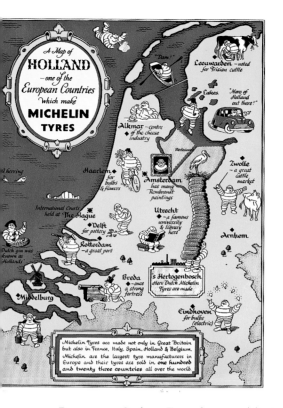

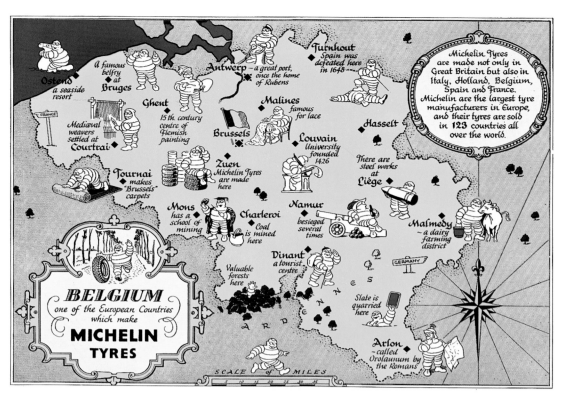

Pyrenees. Only a Frenchman oblivious to the delights of the table would think of travelling by car without this substantial red tome in his glove compartment".

Over the ensuing decades the guide became virtually a national institution. The mobility of the population became ever greater, heralding an age of mass migrations and the creation of a new kind of road, the motorway, specially designed for comfort and speed. These twin-lane highways, introduced in France from 1962 onwards, met with some resistance at first, as if people felt that their long straight lines, avoiding towns and villages, led nowhere. As the number of holiday-makers rose from 37 percent of the population to 56 percent over the period 1960-1980, there were many who, nostalgic for the grand tours of the old days, with their sense of adventure, discovery and contact with local people, denounced mass tourism as a kind of warfare with devastating consequences: "There is nowhere to stay anymore. All we have are collective invasions or individual raids", lamented travel writer Paul Morand in 1967, perpetuating that very human tradition of longing for a lost paradise, spoiled for ever by unending hordes of visitors.

The red guide was renowned for the rigour and integrity of its inspectors, and their anonymous visits were a matter of apprehension for hotel and restaurant owners. For the purposes of the guide Bibendum reined in his natural exuberance. The rubber man, a symbol of quality with respect to tyres, was something of an intruder in this world where punctilious impartiality was the very essence of the guide's inspiration, its methodology, its philosophy, its *raison d'être*. The guide's editorial staff, pragmatic but

incorruptible, for whom advertising, or indeed anything involving payment, was a matter of the greatest distrust, worked out a *modus vivendi* with Bibendum, one that was to be applied with the utmost rigour. His rare appearances were to be channelled, carefully orchestrated and strictly limited to two kinds of activity: the occasional promotional insert, presenting the firm's products - road-maps, or a new tyre - and the guide's practical tips, pages devoted only to information. Here Bibendum could explain the various symbols that categorised a hotel, or the meaning of the colours used to represent roads, and could indicate briefly that a map existed... but no more than that. In this way Bibendum assumed his role as the motorist's friend and adviser, his measured assistance enhancing the guide's content without harming it. This unaccustomed

restraint was essential if the guide's original vocation was to be respected. Its credibility depended on it, as did its strategic function as a vehicle for the company's image -- security, comfort and innovation being values common both to the tyre and to the guide. As a metaphor for the tyre in the world of motoring, the guide is also, in its way, a means for the motorist to make contact with the external environment. In other words, a kind of mini-Bibendum.

Bibendum makes only occasional appearances in the regional tourist guides which have been published since 1926 and in the "red guide". Page 110 and above, top: Series of advertising maps published by Michelin UK, demonstrating the company's international dimension. In each country, Bibendum adopts the local customs.
Right: Bibendum joins in the rage for scooters. Leaflet, 1955.

Bibendum on the beach

Placed on half-rations in the printed press, released on probation in the *Michelin Guide*, Bibendum was seen less often by the French public but, for all that, did not become a recluse. Since 1963 he has joined holiday-makers in their migration to the beaches during the months of July and August. The Michelin caravan hits the road, visiting more than 40 seaside resorts, from Brittany to the Pyrenees, with organisers in Bibendum costumes spreading around the

town to announce to all and sundry the day's programme of games on the beach. The various activities are closely supervised by a team of entertainers whose sole concern is to dazzle the holidaying children with a succession of parades, acrobatics, jazz bands and other cultural events.

The initiative was a roaring success from year one, with the result that additional caravans were sent round other areas of France and Europe, notably Italy, Spain, Germany and Denmark. Each comprised around 40 people, including Michelin employees, students and young teachers and they put on dozens of displays every summer, attracting crowds of up to 3,000 children. These could be seen quietly lined up on the beach in their best clothes, hunched in concentration over a three-dimensional jigsaw which

they were required to put together and to form a Bibendum. Novelist Raymond Las Vergnas (a vice-rector at the Sorbonne and professor of English and American literature) described in one of his crime novels, *Meurtres à Quiberon* (Murder at Quiberon), the atmosphere at one of Bibendum's "beach parties".

"The music boomed out across the sand and hundreds of holiday-makers, grown-ups and children, began appearing from nowhere, as if out of the ground, from elsewhere

on the beach, leaning out of the windows of nearby houses. (...) Two cars, ancient bangers of the kind you see in car museums, had pulled up. On the roof was a large model, the size of a man, swathed in immaculate rings of rubber, swaying gently, waving with his short arms first to the right, then to the left, kicking with his bandaged legs, like a mummy wearing an astronaut's helmet, with a pair of turn-of-the-century motorist's goggles. (...) Then other Bibendums scattered around the beach, all of them cavorting merrily in the best of spirits. One ran down to the beach and began playing ball with the policeman on watch; another tried to mount the beach pony which, despite its professional placidity, displayed signs of an urge to rebel..."

met and there was a dark patch on his bare face. I shouted: He's been killed. He's dead." Bibendum has been foully murdered. Let the inquiry commence...

Michelin developed its programme of beach activities throughout the 1970s. This offset the modesty of its advertising budget in the traditional media and also struck the right chord at a time when motoring was coming within reach of ever greater sections of the population and growing prosperity heralded an era of holidays for all. It indicated too that the right form of publicity had been found for the post-war baby boom. In the 1930s the advertising magazine *Vendre*, finely attuned to developments in advertising in the English-speaking world, had expressed surprise that French business was "neglecting children, the most interesting market for anyone who wants to look to the future. After all, is there any terrain that is more fertile than the mind of a child? (...) How have advertisers gone about attracting the youth market up to now? With few exceptions, with the occasional

Then suddenly some urgent shouts rise above the hubbub of the beach and the novel's heroine, who has been growing bored with having to escort her brother during his rest cure, walks over to the group where the shouts have been coming from. "Half a dozen Bibendums were bustling around a kind of stretcher on which one of their number was laid out. The pseudo-casualty was not wearing his hel-

handout of empty words dressed up in pretty pictures, sometimes at great expense, usually with a lack of conviction. (...) Is this really the best way? Would it not be better, if we wish to reap a rich harvest in the future, to prepare the ground now by planting our seeds judiciously?"

Even in those days, Michelin's tyres were to be found on the model cars that Citroën made for children. Since then, *Vendre*'s comments have been largely taken on board, so much so that that they are now widely regarded

Every summer from 1963, teams of Michelin Men took to the beaches, to the joy of holidaying children. The idea was that when they grew up they would associate Michelin with happy childhood memories.
Page 112, far left: A Bibendum made of shells, built by the child of a company employee.

as self-evident. "The growing influence of young people within the family, their spirit of curiosity and alertness, their keen memory, the tendency of adults to remember their childhood with a rosy glow, all these things encouraged us to set up our beach parties", *Bib*, Michelin's in-house magazine wrote in 1964.

Bibendum's tremendous popularity today undoubtedly owes a great deal to the Michelin beach parties and the decision to view them as a long-term initiative. "We believed that to associate Michelin with a happy period of one's childhood would weigh in our favour later on when, as motorists, these young people might have to make a choice between two brands of tyre", one of the organisers of the operation recalled.

The games on the beach, attracting thousands of happy holiday-making children by the seaside, are one of the last vestiges of the post-war fashion for promotional events on the scale of fairs and shows designed to draw the public in large numbers. Typical of these gatherings were the Children's Fair of 1948 or the Sports and Camping Show of 1950, and of course the annual motor shows, with their enticing displays of the latest in motoring pleasure for the greater delight of their family visitors. These events, attracting large numbers of people to a single location on a fixed date, provided a kind of communion which today, as we prepare to enter the 21st century, would appear exotic. Leisure and the pur-

suit of happiness nowadays tend to involve a return to rural roots, the search for calm and authenticity, trekking through the countryside on foot or mountain bike, well off the beaten track.

Tour de France

The major event of modern times in which Bibendum bonds with the crowds is the Tour de France, the epic cycle race which has itself assumed mythic proportions and which attracts millions of enthusiasts every year. This latter-day Odyssey, conducted in several stages over a period of three weeks, is a fascinating blend of heroism, guile, poetry and tragedy. Launched in 1903, the Tour has become a landmark feature of French popular culture. Needless to say, it has attracted the attention of advertisers who, since the 1930s, have each year formed a fleet of publicity vehicles travelling ahead of the competitors. Many of these vehicles are specially designed for the event, extravagantly large advertising hoardings which aim for maximum effect. It is a loud and brash form of marketing, less favoured now than in the past, promoting a variety of products amid the hubbub of street noise, music and megaphone announcements. As the caravan passes through the various towns and villages along the

route, the crowds of spectators receive a flood of souvenir key-rings, beer-mats, sets of playing cards and peaked caps, all bearing the brand-names of consumer products.

In 1973 Michelin, a regular participant, paraded some vintage cars from the turn of the century: a

Brasier, a Hotchkiss and especially an ancient fire-engine from which Bibendum, perched on the firefighters' ladder, waved graciously to spectators before going on to perform the stunt that was to become a favourite with the crowds in subsequent years: travelling the route between stages, standing upright on his motorcycle, arms aloft. "In his white costume, Michelin's Bibendum was the main attraction of the Tour caravan", wrote the daily *Sud-Ouest*. "He provides a tremendous spectacle and entertains the crowds." The man inside the mascot, Philippe Chapuis, was a former French roller-skating champion and his balancing act was a source of wonderment to spectators. Between 1973 and 1989, the year that Michelin discontinued its participation, Chapuis completed 17 Tours de France, covering some 60,000 miles in all, an outsize performance entirely in keeping with Bibendum's personality.

Between 1973 and 1989, Michelin sent replicas of the vintage Brasier and Hotchkiss motor cars and a fire-engine to take part in the Tour de France cycle race. Spectators were invariably impressed by Bibendum, who covered the course standing upright, arms extended, on the back of a motorcycle.
Page 116: An unusual example of a free interpretation of the Michelin mascot. French poster, 1967.

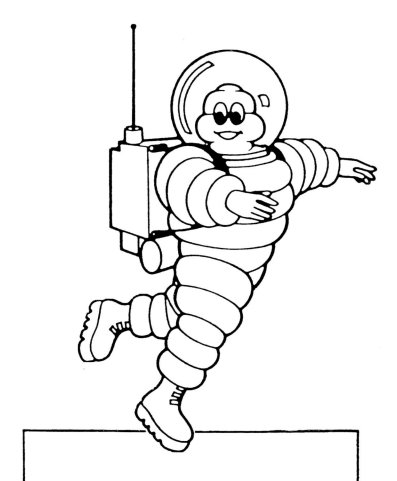

Chapter 7

Bibendum
rides
again

An opinion poll on the French public's favourite companies published by *L'Expansion* magazine in August 1996 showed Michelin in second place behind Chanel and ahead of Mercedes-Benz, which ranked third, BMW (sixth) and Coca-Cola (ninth). For a tyre producer to rank with a legendary fashion house is an astonishing achievement that owes everything to the magic of Bibendum. Quite apart from the entertainment provided in his publicity appearances, Bibendum has always been regarded with tremendous affection in France, the result of the closeness of his relationship with the public, a unique phenomenon in the history of advertising.

The case of the false Bibendum

Foremost among Bibendum's admirers are those knights of the road, the long-distance lorry-drivers. For many, their lives at the wheel have been spent with a Bibendum mounted on the front hood of their trucks, a lucky mascot

one time I got through customs with the paperwork all done in a matter of seconds because of Bibendum and a customs official who thought the same way I did." Another driver, who said he preferred to buy a Michelin map than a newspaper, "a lot more attractive with all those colours". Bibendum represents "a protective shield of the road", a benevolent guardian who everyone doesn't hesitate to personalise by painting. Bibendum-painting in Germany, where the company has been established since 1931, can take highly imaginative forms, as exemplified in the 1986 publication *The Lorry Driver's Dream: Coloured Dolls*. In their introduction, photographer Hans-Rüdiger Strey and sociologist Willy Klawe note the very specific role played by these personalised mascots: they serve as an

to guard over their fortunes. "I drove my lorry for more than 20 years", one driver said. "I always had my Bibendum perched a top my cab, because I like the character and especially because I particularly wanted to give free publicity to a marvellous company. For me, Michelin is France, and I don't think I'm the only one to think that way. I remember

assertion of individual difference, while at the same time stressing their membership to the clan of lorry drivers with its inherent values of freedom, independence and solidarity.

The plastic Bibendum mascot, distributed free by agents to their favourite clients, retailers or drivers, became so successful that an illegal trade in Michelin Men developed, as was revealed one day by an incident on a Dutch motorway. A heavy goods vehicle was driving along

Attached to the radiator grill or to the roof of the driver's cab, the mascot symbolised their spirit of independence and freedom and the solidarity that binds the community of lorry drivers.

the motorway when the Bibendum mascot broke free from its attachment and shattered the windscreen of a motor-car that was following. The driver of the car, a journalist, was unharmed and he later called the Dutch subsidiary's publicity manager in order to show him the miscreant Bibendum which he had recovered from the roadside. The Michelin mascot proved to be a crude forgery which had been badly mounted on the lorry's cab. A private detective was hired to track down the source of the fake. The sleuth discovered that a plastics factory in the Netherlands had been distributing large numbers of fake Michelin Men to garages around Northern Europe for the past several months. As a result, Michelin decided it would produce and sell its own mascots in order to control the quality and distribution. The makers of the fakes -- who had been delivering their false Bibendums by the trailer-load to Britain -- were taken to court and convicted. Another producer of false Michelin Men, based in Turkey, was raided by police some time later.

Japan and the United States. The main symptom was a fervent desire to collect the Michelin brand's editorial and advertising material, ranging from maps to ceramic plaques, from marketing brochures to tourist guides. The longest-standing Michelin fanatic is probably Pierre Métayer, a 54-year-old chef who has been tracking down and collecting Michelin-related material for the past three decades. He caught the bug from his father-in-law who, one day in 1970, handed him an undeveloped roll of photographic film. On developing the film, he found it contained a set of unique photographs dating back to the early 1930s. They recorded a series of tests conducted in Normandy by Pierre's father-in-law and a team of fellow Michelin employees, trying out the prototype of a railcar on tyres, later to become famous under the name Micheline.

"These outstanding images excited my curiosity and from that day the Michelin brand name entered my life and has not left it since", Pierre Métayer confesses. "I don't think a weekend has gone by without my wife and

"Monsieur Michelin"

Fakes of famous brands often become collector's items and become absurdly valuable. Thus from the early 1980s, items relating to Bibendum began to attract the attention of collectors and the phenomenon spread to the extent that the value of Michelin publicity items increased ten-fold. "Michelin-mania" spread around the world, with particularly intense epidemics in France,

I heading off somewhere to track down a new item." Nicknamed "Monsieur Michelin" by antique dealers from one end of the country to the other, Pierre tried to put into words the fascination he felt for the brand-name and the vast collection of items that he has amassed. "Advertising must have been a company obsession, and probably cost them a fortune. They did so many things, some of them I'm still discovering. The subject is extraordinarily rich."

Antigua

The progress they've made in Antigua since the days of Christopher Columbus! A huge airport, intensive sugar-cane cultivation, the most expensive private club in the world, and also, also, the most modern tyre in the world, the Michelin X!

Bibendum

Who is this mysterious traveller and why is he so passionate about Michelin's radial tyre? Is he one of the firm's travelling salesmen? Or maybe a collector? We'll never know, but it is typical of the advertising devices that so enchant Pierre Métayer, who over a period of 27 years has tracked down more than 8,700 Michelin items and documents, constituting an absolutely unique collection. Rejecting offers from Japanese and American

After 27 years of chasing Michelin memorabilia, from garage signs to air pumps, from limited-edition Michelin ashtrays to post-cards, from pressure gauges to boxes of talc for inner tubes, Pierre Métayer has amassed a vast fund of knowledge and a stock of revealing anecdotes testifying to Bibendum's astounding popularity. Among these, one of the most noteworthy and enigmatic is a series of six post-cards sent to a certain M. Daguan in the northern city of Lille. The writer, corresponding with a friend, appears to be tracing the itinerary of Christopher Columbus as he made his way round the Caribbean region on his journeys of 1492 and 1493. Each of the cards, representing views of the Virgin islands, Antigua or Marie-Galante, praises the merits of the Michelin X tyre and is signed: Bibendum. For example:

Dominican Republic

I was surprised by the number of motor cars to be found on the island. The Michelin X tyre is very popular here. Users are able to cover twice as many kilometres in spite of the poor condition of the roads. Great savings!

Bibendum.

Virgin Islands

Famous, famous, famous, famous Michelin X tyres. Famous! That's what the parrots here would say if they could speak!

Bibendum

Michelin-maniacs, he recently decided to donate the collection to Michelin "so that it will never be broken up". Insisting on packing the collection himself, he filled no fewer than 113 cardboard boxes which it took two large lorries to transport. And no sooner had they reached Clermont-Ferrand than "Monsieur Michelin" was out on the road again, sniffing out those precious

Forming part of the popular cultural heritage, Bibendum is appropriated in all kinds of moving ways. In Africa or India, for example, garage or petrol station owners may reinterpret him after their own fashion.
Page 122: Painted walls at Libreville (Gabon).
Page 122, right: Shop sign, Pondicherry (India).
Above: The meeting of two myths, Michelin Man on a Citroën 2CV which -- unknown to most people -- was devised by Pierre Michelin (1903-37), Edouard Michelin's second son, who was joint managing director until his death in a road accident in 1937.
Right, from top down: In Sicily (Italy), this vestige of the Temple of Jupiter on the ancient site of Agrigente is nicknamed "Bibendum", as is this rock in the forest of Nemours, southeast of Paris.

Michelin mascots, combing the antique stalls from north to south and from east to west. "There are still plenty more pieces out there. I know it. I can feel it", he says. For Pierre Métayer the Bibendum of the 1920s represents the peak of advertising achievement, "with his elegance and his eternal cigar... An absolute masterpiece".

Bibendum's new lease on life, independent of the Michelin company, has helped to raise him to the status of a popular hero, one who over and above his marketing role is a reflection of popular values. This has also been confirmed by the various studies on the mascot's semantic content commissioned by the company. Whether carried out in Japan, the United States or France, these studies demonstrate that, despite cultural differences, the ways in which Bibendum is perceived display a high degree of homogeneity. "Friendly", "warm", "smiling", "honest"... these are the words that are invariably used to describe his character. "Bibendum personalises the company and at the same time conveys the benefits that the consumer can expect of it: confidence", one expert noted. He concluded that the mascot was "a good genie", around whom "nothing bad can happen". Yet however reassuring his good humour may appear, Bibendum's rotundity inspires varying reactions. In the United States, his obesity is seen as a handicap. In Japan, on the other hand, the cult of Sumo wrestling means that Bibendum is seen -- particularly by young women -- as a "sporty type", or as "an aristocrat who lives in a castle", or maybe as "an elegant man of the West".

The tyres that save

Secret agent 007 has been laid low with a blow to the head. James Bond, played here by Roger Moore, sprawls across the back seat of a Rolls-Royce driven by the slender-legged Grace Jones, escorted by the muscle-bound Dolph Lundgren, a couple who are undoubtedly to be regarded as a thoroughly bad lot. The car enters a forest and pulls up by a lake. The driver and her companion get out and release the handbrake, sending the Rolls on its way to the bottom of the lake. The luxury vehicle sinks slowly beneath the surface, apparently consigning our hero to a watery grave. The two villains -- KGB agents, naturally -- stand watching from the shore, ready to fire off a round of shots in the unlikely event that Her Majesty's special agent should somehow escape from his motorised coffin. But Bond, as ever, has a trick or two up his sleeve: he succeeds in escaping from his persecutors by breathing the air contained in the car's tyres which, the spectator can clearly read on their sides, are Michelin tyres-- the tyres that save.

This sequence from the Bond movie "A View to a Kill" is typical of a recent trend in advertising known as product placement. Originating in the United States, the practice involves advertisers contributing to a film's production costs in exchange for having their products prominently displayed at some suitable point in the film. The result is a relatively inexpensive visual quotation, often highly effective when the film is a success as was the case for the Bond film.

This rare incursion into the pitiless world of cinema espionage was the occasion for a poster published specially for the movie's American release. It presented Roger Moore and Bibendum standing back to back, arms crossed in the famous pose patented by special agent 007. The poster was designed by Walter Storozuk, then chief artistic designer for Michelin's advertising in the United States. He brought a new approach to Bibendum which shook up the classic image of the brand's logo, the famous symbol, used since the 1930s, of the rubber man rolling a tyre ahead of him, his right hand raised in welcome.

From the 1980s onwards, a Bibendum design by Walter Storozuk began to gain currency within the company as an alternative that could modernise the brand's image. Published two years earlier during the annual convention of

Page 124: *The promotion of car accessories meant that the mascot was often adapted according to climate conditions in the countries involved.*
From top down: *German advertisement, 1959. Poster portraying Bibendum back to back with James Bond for the release of the film "A View to a Kill", by Walter Storozuk, to which Michelin contributed, 1985. Belgian advertisement, 1988. Above, left to right: Running Bib, and the Asian version of the corporate logo, the company's official imprint on all communications. British campaign, 1982.*

In a recent independent survey of car owners, Michelin scored the highest marks for good road holding and handling.
Twice as many as the next highest ranked make of tyre.
Switch to **MICHELIN** and insist on no other.

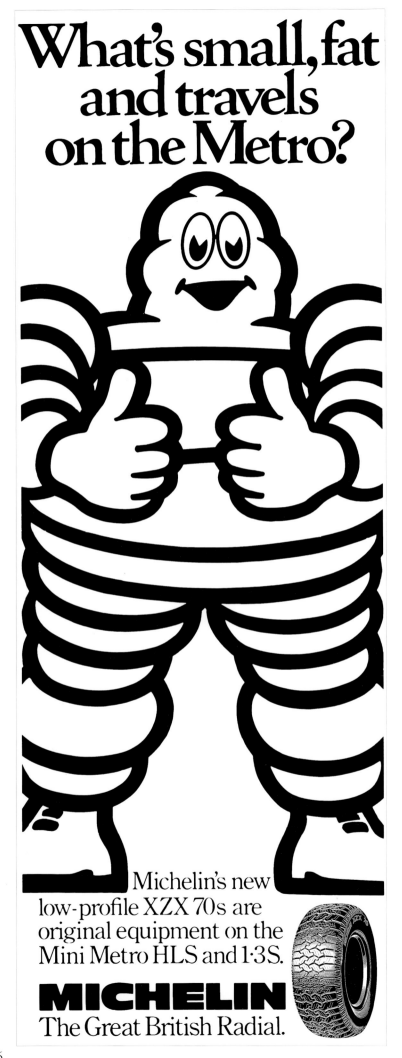

What's small, fat and travels on the Metro?

Michelin's new low-profile XZX 70s are original equipment on the Mini Metro HLS and 1·3S.

MICHELIN

The Great British Radial.

Michelin salesmen in the United States, the design, one of a large number of sketches produced by Storozuk, showed Bibendum face-on in a running posture. Instantly dubbed the "Running Bib", he appeared sleeker, more youthful, more dynamic, determined and powerful. "Over the course of his life, he has been represented in a variety of different ways", Walter Storozuk commented. "He's been drawn both slim and fat, sometimes with a corpulence that makes him look like a balloon. I've given him an appearance which I think conveys an impression of strength, suppleness and a jovial nature, applicable to all sorts of situations. He appears neither too imposing, which would make him overbearing, nor too frail, which would hardly be flattering for the tyre industry."

In Britain, at around the same time, a major publicity campaign was launched presenting Bibendum in heroic guise. Elsewhere, the rubber man remained in purgatory, at least in advertising terms, making little more than fleeting appearances on stickers. For some Michelin advisers, the age and the permanence of the company mascot had become a handicap, associating the brand name with a by-gone age. But others disagreed, and for these Bibendum's renaissance in the United States was an inspiration. Far from being exhausted or petrified, the character displayed a potential that remained fertile, capable of change and of conveying an image of modernity and vitality, providing an example worthy of emulation.

With Bibendum apparently set on a new career in the United States, the group now faced the urgent need to rethink the company emblem. In 1985 it embarked on this overhaul by simultaneously launching a corporate publicity campaign and a drive to re-style the company logo. Among the enthusiasts of the "Running Bib" there were some who were all for adopting him as the new logo; this however, was ruled out. For all the dynamism that emanated from Walter Storozuk's design, the fact remained that it failed to represent a tyre, the company's very *raison d'être*. Others noted that the new "action man" image lacked any connotations of public service, an aspect that Michelin particularly cherished. Moreover, the fist that "Running Bib" thrust before him in his dynamic pose, slightly magnified by the effect of perspective, expressed too much aggression to be appropriate for corporate use. Having reached this decision, the company asked its studio designers to return to the old logo and to come up with a variation that would modernise the image.

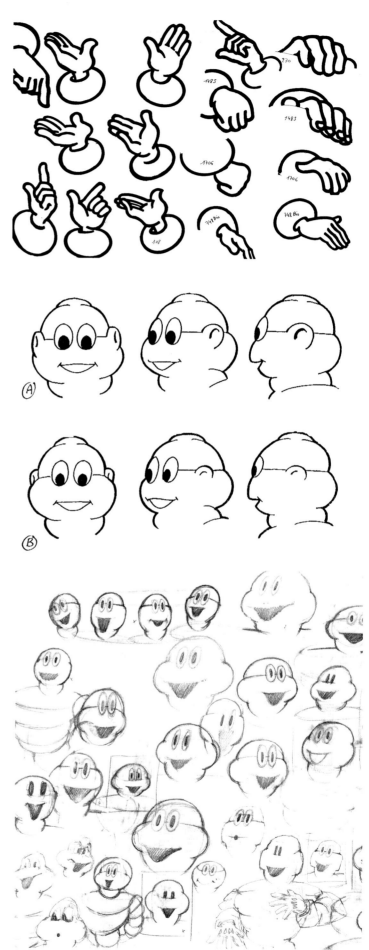

Page 126: From earth-moving machines to the space shuttle, the company name can be found on virtually anything that moves, a fact of which Bibendum is justifiably proud. British advertisement highlighting the use of Michelin tyres on the Mini Metro.
Above: Cartoon sketches, studies of movement and posture, abandoned drafts aimed at providing the mascot with ears.

Vendu dans 3000 pointures.

L'an 2000 déjà atteint.

NOVO MICHELIN 4X4. UM COMPORTAMENTO EXEMPLAR NA CIDADE OU NO CAMPO.

Most of their efforts concentrated on Bibendum's face. His pupils were made rounder, as were his spectacles, which now more resembled those of his American counterpart. The decision was taken to remove the least pleasing aspect of the old logo, the black hole of his mouth which appeared unattractive and troubling. Focusing on this and on a modification of the neckline, the designers produced a silhouette which was more anthropomorphic, with some of the deformations inherent in his tyre-man origins toned down. The new logo, which also stylised the tyre-sculpture, did not alter the fundamentals of the old design, to the disappointment of some who would have preferred a more radical transformation. But that had never been the objective. The idea was to reaffirm the firm's dynamism, but without recasting the image so drastically that all documents, logo-bearing items or Michelin vehicles around the world would require immediate replacement. Such an operation would have cost an estimated 1.5 billion francs (150 million pounds at the 1997 exchange rate).

Evolution not revolution, changing the image while leaving it essentially the same, months of work spent on redesigning a mouth, or altering the carriage of the head...

The use of humour in advertising is a hazardous exercise that agencies often resort to in order to win over consumers who regard the purchase of tyres as a necessary evil.
Above and across: *This poster campaign, signalling Bibendum's return as a major figure in French advertising, introduced a new technique based on innovation and the long-lasting quality of the products, 1986.*
Left: *"City gear you can wear in the country", a Portuguese advertisement for the 4-wheel-drive range, 1994.*

2 milliards
de roues
conquises.

Concerns that may appear outrageously trivial, unworthy of a major company, but which testify to the meticulous attention brought to Bibendum, a precious legacy that was not to be tampered with lightly. It was essential to hold on to that heritage, whatever the difficulties.

As the company's official ambassador in all its communications, the Bibendum logo had to be handled with infinite precaution. However, when it came to advertising, an activity based on shifting contingencies and objectives that were subject to change, the same considerations did not apply. When in 1985 it was decided to launch a campaign that would rejuvenate the company's image in France, the momentous decision was also taken to call in an advertising agency. This was a radical departure from former practice, revolutionary for a firm like Michelin which since its foundation had been proudly independent of the agencies, resorting only to independent graphic designers and its own in-house advertising studio.

The announcement that Michelin was to recruit an outside agency sent shock waves through the advertising world. The prospect of obtaining such a prestigious account had directors and designers scratching their heads to find ways of meeting the challenge: what was the best way to update the image of a century-old firm which, though widely respected, was also seen as set in the traditions of another age? The

agency BDDP, selected against keen competition, launched a campaign in 1986 which introduced some startling innovations in its use of the Michelin mascot: close-ups of a foot, or of a hand, or of the face -- pieces of Bibendum presented against a background of primary colours. For the first time too, his outline was doubled as if new energies ran through him. These forceful images were accompanied by slogans that brought new facts to the attention of the public. For example: "Sold in three thousand sizes"; or "Three hundred ways of saying Tyre"; or "Two billion wheels won over..."

The new campaign had the specific purpose of conveying the impression of dynamism and strength at a time when Michelin needed to make the most of its technological advance and its many years of production experience. With the globalisation of the market, the scores of small producers of the early days had been whittled down to a handful of major companies capable of carrying out the costly research and investment programmes needed to come up with ever more competitive products. Tyres had evolved considerably since the turn of the century, in terms both of their construction and performance and of their durability. In the United States, where the low speed limits and rarity of sharp bends in the road mean that tyres do not wear out so quickly, Michelin has recently launched the

Page 130, bottom, and above: *With his resemblance to a sumo wrestler, Biben-dum is often seen in Japan as a sporting hero. In 1989, Michelin launched this corporate campaign detailing the company's activities in Japan, its third produc-tion centre in Asia.*
Page 130, top: *Japanese campaign for the "green" tyre, 1994.*
Right, from top down: *Korean advertisement, 1994. Bust for Japanese retail outlets.*

XH4, the first tyre whose guarantee of 80,000 miles corresponds to the life expectancy of the vehicle itself. This considerable increase in the tyre's durability has meant that the product has come more and more to be taken for granted. With the need for replacement arising less frequently (other than in accidents), it no longer forms one of the consumer's main preoccupations. Nowadays most consumers, apart from connoisseurs obsessed with performance, regard having to buy a set of tyres as a constraint, a necessary evil, the unexpected expenditure creating an unwelcome burden.

How do you sell a tyre? "Unlike the motor car, the tyre -- and this is an understatement -- is the object of nobody's desires and there is some difficulty involved in promoting it", a BDDP consultant on the Michelin account noted. With a product generally perceived as banal, advertisers can choose one of two options: to play it for laughs, put on a show and thus acquire a reputation for the brand name that will impress itself in the minds of the public, or, as was decided with Michelin, to tackle the problem head-on, to try to overcome the obstacles and "debanalise" the product by demonstrating its astonishing complexity -- which need not in itself exclude a touch of humour.

An example of the head-on approach was the 1987 television advertisement that demonstrated the ability of the MX tyre to disperse water at the rate of more than five gallons per second. With technical demonstrations of this kind the role of Bibendum is minimal and it was only in 1992 that the mascot made a proper come-back, in a series of

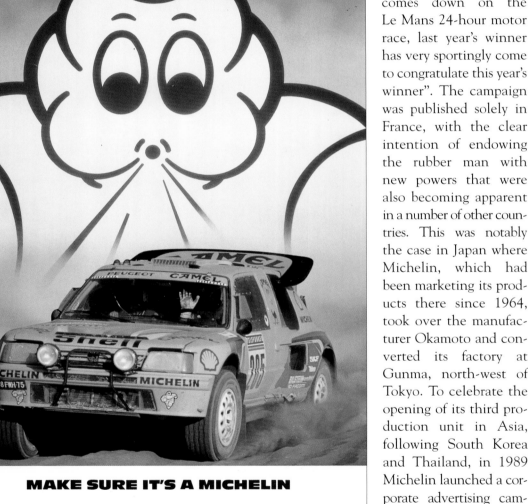

MAKE SURE IT'S A MICHELIN

advertisements hailing Michelin's victories in various competitions. Published in the daily press, they returned to the humour of the early years, exploiting the character's extraordinary vigour and demonstrating that, nearly a century on, he has lost none of his legendary bravado. One of the ads portrayed two Michelin Men shaking hands and smiling broadly, with the slogan: "As the curtain comes down on the Le Mans 24-hour motor race, last year's winner has very sportingly come to congratulate this year's winner". The campaign was published solely in France, with the clear intention of endowing the rubber man with new powers that were also becoming apparent in a number of other countries. This was notably the case in Japan where Michelin, which had been marketing its products there since 1964, took over the manufacturer Okamoto and converted its factory at Gunma, north-west of Tokyo. To celebrate the opening of its third production unit in Asia, following South Korea and Thailand, in 1989 Michelin launched a corporate advertising campaign of exceptional graphic purity, in which Bibendum taught the Japanese public to pronounce the company name by means of phonetic signs.

The same year Michelin, by now the world leader in the tyre market, set about unifying its media campaigns by asking two advertising consultancy groups to take charge of the company's advertising worldwide. Europe, the Middle East and Africa were to be handled by BDDP in Paris, while the Americas, South Africa and Asia were entrusted

Quelle joie pour les parents
de pouvoir compter 6 Champions de France
dans la famille.

Michelin. Champion de France Moto 1993,
750 Promosport, 600 Supersport (national et international),
400, 250, et 125 Promosport.

MICHELIN

Les Championnats de France Moto Promosport et
pneumatiques utilisés sont strictement de série.
125, 250, 400, 750 Promosport et 600 Supersport,
moto les pneumatiques vainqueurs TX11 et TX23
Cagiva, Honda, Kawasaki, Suzuki et Yamaha.
à la technologie Michelin, et bien sûr aux vainqueurs : Stéphane Chambon (125 Cagiva), Didier Rossi (250 Suzuki),
Jérome Alazard (400 Kawasaki), Juan-Eric Gomez (750 Suzuki), Thierry Autissier et Rachel Nicotte (600 Supersport Honda).

600 Supersport sont des épreuves où les motos et
Champion de France 1993 dans les catégories
Michelin vous offre la possibilité de monter sur votre
(gommes A ou B), qui équipent notamment
Bravo à tous les concurrents qui ont fait confiance

N° 1 EN COMPÉTITION, N° 1 EN TECHNOLOGIE.

BIB, BIB, HURRA!

MICHELIN

r ist der große Star im internationalen Motorsport: dieser
leine, charmante Franzose, der mit vollem Namen Bibendum
eißt. Er steht für Michelin, und Michelin-Reifen haben auch
988 wieder einen Erfolg nach dem anderen eingefahren:
latz 1 beim Würth Super-Cup für Sportwagen, Platz 2
ei der Sportwagen-Weltmeisterschaft (beides: Schlesser

auf Sauber Mercedes), Platz 1 bei der Rallye-Weltmeister
schaft (Biasion/Siviero auf Lancia Integrale). Und auch be
der Motorrad-WM hatte Michelin die Nase vorn, und dar
in allen Klassen: in der 500er (Lawson auf Yamaha), de
250er (Pons auf Honda), der 125er und der 80er (beide
Martinez auf Derbi). Wenn das kein Grund zum Jubeln ist

MICHELIN
TECHNOLOGIE VON MICHELIN. DER KONSEQUENTE WEG ZUR SICHERHEIT.

BESPAAR
200 LITER OP
50 000 KM.

NIEUW
MICHELIN
ENERGY
VERDER MET MINDER ENERGIE.

Page 132: *From the very start Michelin's history has been linked with
motor racing, considered to stimulate research. Since 1980 the firm has
been actively involved in the world rally championship.*
Above left: *From 1992, this press campaign marked a return to the
humour of the early years. "What a pleasure for parents to have six
French champions in the family", advertisement hailing Michelin's
victories in the French motorcycle championships, 1993.*
Above right: *German advertisement presenting the trophy offered to the
winners of Michelin-sponsored competitions.*
Right: *Bibendum's contours become a metaphor for the road, European
launch campaign for the Energy tyre, 1994.*

to the DDB agency in New York. Each of these groups was to prepare major transnational campaigns that would be implemented within individual countries by means of specific actions designed by their local agencies. It was within this context that the decision was taken to allow Bibendum to play an increasingly prominent role. And this was the policy adopted in 1994, in the group's first international campaign aimed at launching Michelin's new Energy range, when Europe was subjected to a unique press and television campaign. What made it stand out was the way it managed both to spell out the uniqueness of the tyre and its revolutionary petrol-saving silica-based composition and to place the company mascot at the heart of its campaign. It achieved this most ingeniously, in the advertisement devised by BDDP, by means of a metaphor. The film portrayed the tyre progressing along a twisting road which then turns out to be made up of Bibendum's bands.

Henceforth, Bibendum began to reappear systematically all around the world. He showed up in Korea, in Malaysia, in Hong Kong on those huge hoardings that have made the former British colony a publicity man's

paradise. He slipped into an elegant kimono to appear on the Japanese stage, while in Switzerland, Austria, Germany and other northern European countries he donned a ski-cap and woolly scarf to promote snow-tyres. In Australia, promoting a range of tyres adapted to tropical rains, he wore deep-sea diving goggles. The posters sported the slogan first used in the United States: "Because so much is riding on your tyres". Bibendum is also to be found on Israeli buses, on the display shelves of Pakistani garage-owners, on road-signs in Brazil, Turkey, China or Polynesia, on the neon signs of retailers in Dubai or Abu Dhabi... Bibendum is on the move, taking over advertising spaces around the world.

While substantial sums of money are being invested in enhancing the presence and prestige of Bibendum in the world's markets, the company appears undecided as to how to use the "Running Bib", if at all, and how to pitch the corporate image. Which representation of Bibendum is to be preferred in advertising? Reluctant to choose between the traditionally reassuring Bibendum and the more combative "Running Bib", the company is paying the price of the joint success of its two versions of the mascot, both of which have met with public approval. And so each of them pursues his separate career, one replacing the other according to the country and the nature of the campaign. The paradox, revealing as it is, is only apparent, reflecting the nature of a character who all through the century has swung back and forth between impertinence and benevolence, between diatribes against the competition or the authorities on the one hand and easy-going advice and assistance to motorists on the other. Reassuring and overbearing, wise-talking and trouble-making, Bibendum's dual nature is a perfect reflection of the parent company, the fiercely independent Michelin for whom tradition and modernity are inextricably linked. For the worst, according to some communications experts who would like to unify the mascot once and for all on the lines of Coca Cola's campaign; for the better according to others, who see Michelin as a text-book case of a hybrid brand image both rich and original, to be maintained and cherished. Seen in this light, Bibendum's future appears to be doubly assured. "In the coming years, we plan to have him play a much greater role", the BDDP agency says. "He is the symbol that represents the brand and distinguishes it from all others, the perfect federating agent for all its industrial and editorial activities."

It is clear, therefore, that Bibendum still has a long career ahead of him and that he will continue to perform, to a large extent by popular demand. It would be instructive to list all the varied and unexpected tributes that have been paid to him, for example the several paintings by Salvador Dali, and those of another painter, Alfred Courmes, who prefigured the Pop Art of the 1930s, joyfully mixing Christian iconography, Greek and Roman mythology and advertising imagery. In two paintings Courmes represents Bibendum holding a lily in his hand, a symbol of purity and innocence and of the choice of a loved one, but also, in heraldic imagery, of the wheel, the sun and the world. Closer to present times, the 1980s were a time of free expression for anonymous urban artists who opted to make their mark on walls, using cardboard cut-outs to leave stencilled images, including an army of Bibendums, around the city. Around the same time a number of cartoonists saw new graphic opportunities in the rubber man, notably the Spanish artist Javier Mariscal, who made him the hero of one of his strips. Since 1988 another artist, Fabrice Hybert, has produced a series of works in which Bibendum is a major theme. He sees the Michelin mascot as an archetype. "Bibendum is my

favourite character", he says. "At a time when the telephone and the Internet enable people to travel round the world at the push of a button, he is the character who best symbolises the principle of movement. He is no longer a form of transport, he is transport itself. (...) He's a fairy-tale character whom I often place alongside, or in conversation with, Father Christmas, another character who is able to whizz round the world carrying his sack of presents. Together they form a mythical couple in which Father Christmas is of course the father, and Bibendum the child."

Inevitably there are those hardcore nostalgics who regret that "Bibendum isn't the man he used to be", sighing for the days of Bibendum's Havana cigar and boots. It goes entirely without saying that Bibendum is not what he used to be. It is precisely this quality that has enabled him to defy the years: his ability to adapt to the spirit of the changing times. At the turn of the century, embarking on his career, he reflected perfectly the eccentricities of the motorists of the time, the well-to-do pioneers pursuing a life of thrills and spills. His mimetic talents undiminished by time, he now appears a less disturbing figure, more civilised and more in tune with the image of today's motor car -- an everyday object

Bibendum as a motif in the world of art.
Page 134, from top down: *Forceful Bibendum as seen by artist France de Ranchin, 1997. Stencil on a Paris wall, 1982.*
Top: *A typical "assemblage" by Salvador Dali, one of two statuettes blending a bird with Bibendum's lower parts, "surrealist sculpture" circa 1970.*
Centre: *Bibendum seen by the illustrator Pierre Le Tan, 1979.*

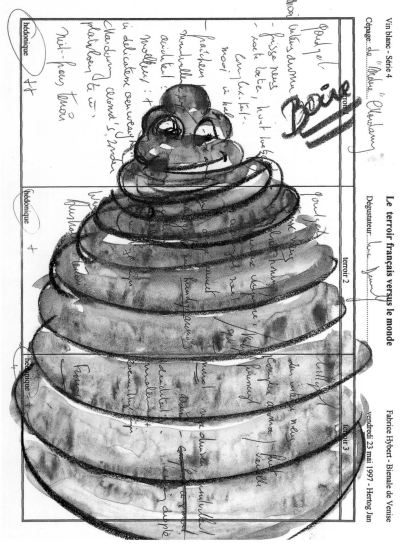

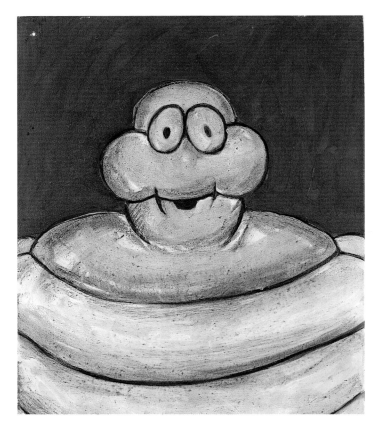

that arouses more rational expectations. The dream of the new *homo automobilis* is no longer to be a horseman without horses but, more pragmatically, to enjoy his or her vehicle as a high-performance tool, a means of getting about in comfort and safety. Accompanying the progress of the Michelin tyre company to its front-rank position in world markets, the "drinker of obstacles" has seen his responsibilities increase vastly. He continues to provide rubber tyres for the wheels of the latter-day Charles Terronts, but also for the wheels of metro coaches, of aircraft, of space shuttles -- indeed of everything that runs on wheels. And Bibendum continues to bestride the world, having learnt the sad lesson of those long-gone mascots of yesteryear who failed to evolve. On he strides to new adventures, adapting to the needs of the times, ready for anything, etched forever in the popular memory, assured of his place in advertising's hall of fame.

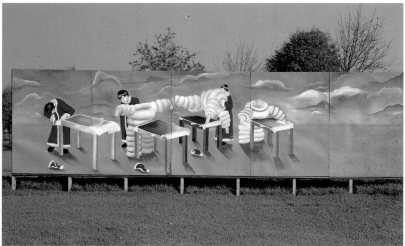

In 1988, sculptor Fabrice Hybert made Bibendum one of the central themes of his work.
Top left: A picture sketched during the 1997 Venice biennial.
Right: "Portrait of the Inflatable Man", 1988.
Bottom, and page 137, bottom: The artist often pairs together Father Christmas and Bibendum, hoardings, 1995-1997.
Vignette: In the 1970s Bibendum featured regularly in the strip cartoons of Spanish artist Javier Mariscal, his path crossing that of the main protagonists, bohemian hedonists Fermin and Piker.
Page 137, top: Bibendum in Egypt, as imagined by British artist Glen Baxter, 1997.

MICHELIN MUMMY

Joint tribute to Bibendum and Arcimboldo,
German calendar cover, Mirko Illic, 1990.

Acknowledgments

The author wishes to thank all those who have helped or encouraged him in one way or another:
Christel Aguettant, Alain Arnaud, Antoine Barthuel, Aimé Bloton, Philippe Chapuis, Robert Cuzin, Michel Coudeyre, Juliette Darmon, Anne Daubrée, Bruno Delhomme, Didier Derbal, Christian Derouet, Olivier Desgranges, Denis Fischer, Marie-France Fournival, Pierre Gauthronet, Ugo Graglia, Robert Hiebel, Fabrice Hybert, Gonzague de Jarnac, Alain Lachartre, Serge Laget, Jean Laporte, Christian Marmonnier, Pierre Métayer, François Michel, Daniel Michelin, Guy Michelin, Isabelle Morand, Paul Niblett, Victoria Oso Nkuku, Jean Oger, Patrick Oliva, Pierre Pailheret, Bill Patterson, Cyrille Putman, Annick Rouaud, Philippe Rossillon, Jean-Pierre Roudaire, Jean-Claude Salbert, Raymond Savignac, Jean Walter Schleich, Walter Storozuk, Pierre le Tan, Jean-Pierre Vuillerme.
The Michelin teams who helped to revise the translations. And last but not least, the artists and designers without whom *One Hundred Years of Michelin Man* would never have been possible.

Bibliography

PIERRE ALBERT
Histoire de la Presse,
Paris, Presses Universitaires de France, 1970.

Art & Pub,
catalogue of the exhibition Art et Publicité 1890-1990,
Paris, éditions du Centre Georges Pompidou, 1990.

R. BLETTERIE,
Michelin, Clermont-Ferrand, capitale du pneu, 1900-1920,
Avallon, éditions de Civry, 1981.

MARCEL BLEUSTEIN-BLANCHET,
Mémoires d'un lion,
Paris, Librairie Académique Perrin, 1988.

GÉRARD CARON,
Un carré noir dans le design,
Paris, Dunod, 1992.

ALFRED COURMES, *Textes, annotations et interviews par Christian Derouet,* Paris, éditions du Musée de Roubaix, with the assistance of the Berggruen gallery, 1989.

PAUL DERMÉE AND EUGÈNE COURMONT,
Les affaires et l'affiche,
volume 8 in the "Technique des affaires" series, Paris, Dunod, 1922.

DANIEL FABRE,
Carnaval ou la fête à l'envers,
Paris, Gallimard, 1992.

MAX GALLO,
L'affiche, miroir de l'histoire,
Paris, Robert Laffont, 1989.

PIERRE-GABRIEL GONZALEZ,
Bibendum, publicité et objets Michelin,
Paris, Editions du Collectionneur, 1995.

ANDRÉ GUESLIN (director of publication),
Michelin, les hommes du pneu,
Paris, Les éditions de l'Atelier, Editions ouvrières, 1993.

ALAIN JEMAIN,
Michelin, un siècle de secrets,
Paris, Calmann-Levy, 1982.

RAYMOND LAS VERGNAS,
Meurtres à Quiberon,
Paris, Albin Michel, 1967.

ANTOINE LEFEBURE,
Havas, les arcanes du pouvoir,
Paris, Grasset, 1992.

MARC MARTIN,
Trois siècles de publicité en France,
Paris, éditions Odile Jacob, 1992.

RENÉ MIQUEL,
Dynastie Michelin,
Paris, La table ronde, 1962.

HANS-RÜDIGER STREY, WILLY KLAWE,
Bunte Puppen, Truckertraïme,
Hambourg, Christians, 1986.

ALAIN WEILL,
L'affiche française, Paris,
Presses Universitaires de France, 1982.

PERIODICALS
Dailies: *Le Petit Journal, Le Figaro.*
Specialised periodicals: *Vendre, La Publicité, La Publicité Moderne.*

Credits

Table of contents

Printed in June 1998
by Mondadori, Verona
Printed in the EEC